TABITHA

A Play in Three Acts

By Arnold Ridley
and Mary Cathcart Borer

⏐SAMUEL FRENCH⏐

Copyright © 1956 Arnold Ridley and Mary Cathcart Borer
All Rights Reserved

TABITHA is fully protected under the copyright laws of the British Commonwealth, including Canada, the United States of America, and all other countries of the Copyright Union. All rights, including professional and amateur stage productions, recitation, lecturing, public reading, motion picture, radio broadcasting, television, online/digital production, and the rights of translation into foreign languages are strictly reserved.

ISBN 978-0-573-01435-2

concordtheatricals.co.uk

concordtheatricals.com

FOR AMATEUR PRODUCTION ENQUIRIES

UNITED KINGDOM AND WORLD
EXCLUDING NORTH AMERICA
licensing@concordtheatricals.co.uk
020-7054-7298

Each title is subject to availability from Concord Theatricals, depending upon country of performance.

CAUTION: Professional and amateur producers are hereby warned that *TABITHA* is subject to a licensing fee. The purchase, renting, lending or use of this book does not constitute a licence to perform this title(s), which licence must be obtained from the appropriate agent prior to any performance. Performance of this title(s) without a licence is a violation of copyright law and may subject the producer and/or presenter of such performances to penalties. Both amateurs and professionals considering a production are strongly advised to apply to the appropriate agent before starting rehearsals, advertising, or booking a theatre. A licensing fee must be paid whether the title is presented for charity or gain and whether or not admission is charged.

This work is published by Samuel French, an imprint of Concord Theatricals Ltd.

The Professional Rights in this play are controlled by Eric Glass Ltd, 25 Ladbroke Cresent, London W11 1PS.

No one shall make any changes in this title for the purpose of production. No part of this book may be reproduced, stored in a retrieval system, scanned, uploaded, or transmitted in any form, by any means, now known or yet to be invented, including mechanical, electronic, digital, photocopying, recording, videotaping, or otherwise, without the prior written permission of the publisher. No one shall share this title, or part of this title, to any social media or file hosting websites.

The moral right of Arnold Ridley & Mary Cathcart Borer to be identified as authors of this work has been asserted in accordance with Section 77 of the Copyright, Designs and Patents Act 1988.

USE OF COPYRIGHTED MUSIC

A licence issued by Concord Theatricals to perform this play does not include permission to use the incidental music specified in this publication. In the United Kingdom: Where the place of performance is already licensed by the PERFORMING RIGHT SOCIETY (PRS) a return of the music used must be made to them. If the place of performance is not so licensed then application should be made to PRS for Music (www.prsformusic.com). A separate and additional licence from PHONOGRAPHIC PERFORMANCE LTD (www.ppluk.com) may be needed whenever commercial recordings are used. Outside the United Kingdom: Please contact the appropriate music licensing authority in your territory for the rights to any incidental music.

USE OF COPYRIGHTED THIRD-PARTY MATERIALS

Licensees are solely responsible for obtaining formal written permission from copyright owners to use copyrighted third-party materials (e.g., artworks, logos) in the performance of this play and are strongly cautioned to do so. If no such permission is obtained by the licensee, then the licensee must use only original materials that the licensee owns and controls. Licensees are solely responsible and liable for clearances of all third-party copyrighted materials, and shall indemnify the copyright owners of the play(s) and their licensing agent, Concord Theatricals Ltd., against any costs, expenses, losses and liabilities arising from the use of such copyrighted third-party materials by licensees.

IMPORTANT BILLING AND CREDIT REQUIREMENTS

If you have obtained performance rights to this title, please refer to your licensing agreement for important billing and credit requirements.

TABITHA

Produced at the Duchess Theatre, London, on the 8th March, 1956, with the following cast of characters:

(in the order of their appearance)

DR MARTIN BRENTWOOD	*Jack Watling*
JANET BOWERING	*Janet Barrow*
MARY TRELLINGTON	*Anne Leon*
MR FAWCETT	*Morris Sweden*
MRS RUTH PRENDERGAST	*Marjorie Fielding*
MRS ELEANOR TRELLINGTON	*Gillian Lind*
LAVINIA GOLDSWORTHY	*Christine Silver*
DETECTIVE INSPECTOR BRUTON	*Philip Stainton*
DR BROWNLIE, a police surgeon	*Franklyn Scott*

The play directed by HAROLD FRENCH

SYNOPSIS OF SCENES

The action of the Play passes in Janet Bowering's attic bed-sitting-room in the small East Anglian cathedral city of Linchminster

ACT I
5 p.m. on Christmas Eve

ACT II
9 p.m. the same evening

ACT III
11 p.m. the same evening

Time—the present

ACT I

Scene—*Janet Bowering's attic bed-sitting-room in the small East Anglian city of Linchminster. 5 p.m. on Christmas Eve.*

The room is in an apartment house in St Jude's Causeway, a narrow paved passage beside St Jude's Church. It is a clean but shabby room, with a ceiling sloping down to the back wall, in which there are two sash windows overlooking the side of the church, with its big, stained glass window, through which the lights of the Church shine during evening service. There are heavy faded curtains at the windows, but no blinds. Down L is a fireplace, in front of which is a small gas fire with a slot meter. The door to the landing is up L and there is another small opening down R. There is no door to this but the scullery, with tap and sink, is partly concealed by a curtain. Up R stands a cheap, narrow iron bedstead, covered with a faded travelling rug and shabby cushions. The rest of the furniture is just as depressing, a mixture of enamelled deal and one or two clumsy Victorian pieces. Just above the fire, facing front, is a large cupboard. An old-fashioned leather armchair stands in front of the fireplace, and there is a small round table RC, surrounded by three chairs, cheap and all different. There is a chest of drawers between the windows, a glass-fronted china cabinet down R, a small cupboard above the bed, a bedside table, and a wardrobe stands up LC. A kitchen chair stands down L. Sad looking ferns stand on the window ledges. There are a few framed texts and religious water-colours: and in marked contrast, an oil painting of an Edwardian lady over the mantelpiece and a large photograph of a nineteen-fourteen–nineteen-eighteen war second lieutenant complete with sword and gloves. There is a clock on the mantelpiece and various small photographs and cheap ornaments. The linoleum is shabby, the rugs worn. In fact, the whole atmosphere of the room is one of faded gentility. This evening there are small sprigs of holly on the more important pictures: and home-made paper chains add to the pathos of an attempt to establish a festive gaiety. There are Christmas cards, but very few of them, on the mantelpiece. The room is lit by a table-lamp on the bedside table R and two electric wall-brackets with old-fashioned shades, over the mantelpiece. The light switch is below the door up L.

(*See the Ground Plan and Photograph of the Scene*)

When the Curtain *rises, the room is growing dark. The lights are on, but the window curtains are not drawn. Lights burn in St Jude's and the colours of the stained-glass window show clearly. Footsteps and occasional voices are heard from the Causeway below and from the church a choir is practising, accompanied by the organ. The gas fire is lit and*

Janet's nightdress is airing over the back of the kitchen chair which is set in front of the fire. DOCTOR MARTIN BRENTWOOD *is seated* L *of the table, writing a prescription. An open medical bag and a stethoscope are on the table beside him. He is aged about thirty, tall and good-looking, in a manly way, with an air of quiet authority. One can imagine him, during his student days, playing rugger or boxing for his hospital.* JANET BOWERING, *his patient, is standing near the* R *window, looking down. She is a faded round-shouldered, thin little woman of about sixty-five. Her hair, which is greying, is pulled back in a tight, old-fashioned bun. She looks pale and fragile, and her clothes, though neat, are drab and much mended.*

MARTIN (*looking up*) Now then, Miss Bowering. Come away from that window. I'm sure there's a draught.

JANET. It's the carols, Doctor. I do so like to hear them.

MARTIN (*reproving kindly*) I dare say. All the same . . . (*He indicates that she should move*)

JANET (*moving down* R) Besides—I'm better.

MARTIN (*glancing through the prescription he has written*) Yes—but you're not out of the wood yet—and it's bitterly cold. That gas fire's very small for a room this size.

JANET. I did wonder about asking Mrs Trellington for a bigger one—but gas is so expensive—(*she moves up* L *of the table*) and somehow . . .

(MARTIN *hands the prescription to* JANET)

Oh, dear! Not *more* medicine.

MARTIN (*rising*) Only a tonic—something to buck you up. Who's going to fetch it for you?

JANET. I can slip round to Conway's myself.

MARTIN (*decisively*) Oh, no, you can't. Isn't there anyone you can send?

JANET. Well—Miss Goldsworthy's out already, and . . .

MARTIN. Then *I'll* drop it in and get them to deliver it. (*He moves down* R) Christmas Day tomorrow, you know, and I want you to start on this at once.

JANET. But *will* they send it?

MARTIN (*smiling*) Oh—I think so—if I ask them to. (*He moves to* R *of the table, picks up his stethoscope and puts it in his pocket*)

(*There is a knock at the door*)

JANET (*calling nervously*) Who is it?
MARY (*off; calling*) It's only me, Mary.
JANET (*calling*) Oh, come in, Mary.

(MARY TRELLINGTON *enters* L. *She is an attractive girl aged about twenty-five, well but simply dressed, and with great charm of manner*)

MARY (*moving* LC) Well, how's the patient?

MARTIN. Going along nicely. I'm quite pleased with her.
MARY. Splendid! (*To Janet*) I'm sorry to interrupt, Miss Bowering, but Mr Fawcett's called to see you.
JANET (*in a flutter*) Mr Fawcett. Mr Fawcett . . . (*She finishes lamely*)
MARTIN (*smiling*) Mr Fawcett?
JANET. I wonder what he wants.
MARY (*joining in the game*) I must say, I was rather surprised.
MARTIN. Well, I should think so indeed. Mr Fawcett coming up here to a lady's bedroom.
JANET. But he's never been up here before. (*She looks from one to the other, puzzled at first, then a smile breaks*)
MARY. Well, really, Miss Bowering . . .
JANET. You're—you're pulling my leg.
MARY (*laughing*) Shall I ask him to wait?
MARTIN. Oh, no. (*He moves to the bed and picks up his coat*) Mustn't keep Mr Fawcett waiting. I'm off. Oh, by the way, Miss Bowering—those tablets—you've enough left to carry you over the holidays?
JANET. Oh, yes, thank you—plenty.
MARTIN (*moving to* L *of Janet*) Have you indeed? Sure you've been taking them regularly?

(JANET *hesitates*)

MARY. How many have you taken *today*, for instance?
JANET (*crossing to the fireplace*) Well, I'm afraid I'm not very good at swallowing things. Although they're a pretty colour, I admit.
MARTIN. Then let me see you take one at once—while I'm still here.
JANET (*smiling timidly*) Very well, Doctor. (*To Mary*) You're very strict with me, you know. (*She takes a bottle of pills from the mantelpiece*) But I must get some water first.

(JANET *crosses and exits to the scullery.* MARTIN *moves hurriedly to* L *of Mary and takes her hand*)

MARTIN. I was afraid you were out. (*Softly*) It's ages since I saw you.
MARY (*agreeing*) Two whole days.
MARTIN. You're looking wonderful.
MARY. Thank you, darling. About the midnight service—will you be able to come?
MARTIN. Yes. I'll call for you—half past eleven?
MARY. I'd better call for you. You're not very popular with step-mamma.
MARTIN. For the life of me, I can't think why.
MARY. Maybe she thinks your frequent visits here aren't entirely concerned with Miss Bowering's bronchitis.

MARTIN. Supposing they're not? Why should she mind?

MARY. Well, I'm very useful to her about the house and perhaps she guesses that one day, because of you . . .

(JANET *enters from the scullery*)

JANET (*triumphantly*) There!

MARTIN. You've really taken it?

JANET. Cross my heart. (*She moves to the bedside table*) Now, I'll put them here—by my bed—(*she puts the bottle of pills on the bedside table*) so that I shan't forget them. (*She moves up* L *of the table*) Mary dear, if Dr Brentwood must be going, perhaps you'll be kind enough to ask Mr Fawcett to come up?

MARY. Of course I will.

(MARY *crosses and exits* L)

MARTIN (*moving to the door* L) Now take it easy, Miss Bowering, and keep warm. (*He smiles at her*) And don't forget—I'm only round the corner. I can look in any time you want me. Merry Christmas!

JANET. Thank you, Doctor. And the same to you.

(MARTIN *exits* L. JANET, *alone in her attic, looks around, crosses to the armchair* LC, *tidies the cushion on it, then moves to the fire to warm her hands. As she does so, the fire goes out.* JANET *turns off the gas, moves to the chest of drawers up* C, *picks up her handbag, extracts her purse, takes out a shilling to put in the meter, but decides against it, and replaces it in the purse. She puts her handbag down, moves to the chair above the table, picks up her cardigan and puts it on. There is a knock on the door.* JANET *crosses to the fireplace, takes her nightdress from the chair, sets the chair down* L, *crosses to the bed and puts the nightdress under the cover*)

(*She calls*) Come in. (*She moves* C)

(MARY *enters* L *and holds the door open.*

MR FAWCETT *enters* L. *He is a dapper little man aged about sixty, clean-shaven and chubby cheeked. His clothes are those of a small shopkeeper, dark, old-fashioned, but well-kept, for* FAWCETT, *a widower, is a jeweller and antique dealer, doing quite well, in a small way. He is habitually cheerful and takes some delight in being old-fashioned. Several years ago, someone told him he was a "Dickens" type, and he has been trying to live up to it ever since*)

Do come in, Mr Fawcett.

FAWCETT (*moving* LC) Thank you. (*He puffs a bit*) Oh, dear me—the stairs. Not so young as I used to be, I'm afraid.

JANET. No. Er—this *is* a pleasant surprise. How are you?

FAWCETT. How are *you*, Miss Bowering? Mary tells me you've had a touch of bronchitis.

(MARY *exits* L, *closing the door*)

JANET. I'm almost better again now.
FAWCETT. Well, I'm very glad to hear *that*.
JANET (*after a pause*) Do sit down, Mr Fawcett.
FAWCETT. After you. (*He holds the armchair for Janet*) I mustn't stay a minute. Allow me.

(JANET, *a little fluttery, but enjoying herself, sits in the armchair*)

(*He stands* R *of Janet*) Now—before I forget. (*He takes an envelope from his pocket, and with a flourish, hands it to Janet*) The compliments of the season, Miss Bowering.

(JANET *opens the envelope and extracts a Christmas card*)

JANET (*smiling*) Oh, thank you. A robin redbreast, dear little thing. How very kind of you, Mr Fawcett.
FAWCETT (*crossing to* RC; *equally pleased*) Not at all, not at all. I always like to deliver my Christmas cards in person, you know. A little foible of mine. And may I add my best wishes for your complete recovery?
JANET. Thank you, Mr Fawcett. But I really am almost well again. It's just these English winters, you know. When I was with Lady Glassbury—(*she indicates the portrait*) we used to spend the cold months in the South of France.
FAWCETT. Ah, yes. (*He moves above the table*) Nice and Monte, eh? Never been there myself, but I hear it's very—er . . . (*He breaks off*) Oughtn't you to have a fire, perhaps?
JANET. It's only just gone out—and I found I hadn't any spare change.
FAWCETT (*moving to* R *of Janet and jingling some coins in his pocket*) Perhaps I could help? (*He puts his hat on the chest of drawers*)
JANET. Oh, no—please don't bother. I'm *quite* warm enough—if *you* are.
FAWCETT. Oh, yes—yes, of course. (*He glances at the door* L, *then leans forward confidentially*) Dear Mary's looking very pretty these days, isn't she?
JANET. Oh, yes. Such a sweet girl.
FAWCETT (*knowingly*) She and young Dr Brentwood, eh? What do you think?
JANET. I shouldn't be at *all* surprised.
FAWCETT. Nor should I. Very suitable in every way. Mary working at the hospital—in the dispensary. Of course, her stepmother would miss her.
JANET (*a little grimly*) She certainly *would*.
FAWCETT. Poor Mrs Trellington. But she'd be only too glad to see Mary happy, I know. I'm sure it must be a great comfort to you and the other two ladies, to have found accommodation in such a delightful household.

JANET. Oh, yes—we all try to be most grateful.

FAWCETT. D'you know, last October, when I had influenza, Mrs Trellington came in every day and looked after the shop for me—even cooked my meals? It was almost as though my poor, dear wife were back again. (*He paces down* R) Ah, well—if I'm not careful, I shall be forgetting why I called to see you. (*He moves to* R *of Janet*) I have a motive for my visit, you know.

JANET (*apprehensively*) A motive?

FAWCETT. Yes.

JANET. Oh, I'm afraid that I can't ...

FAWCETT (*reading her thoughts*) Oh, no. I'm not collecting for anything. It's an invitation from the Vicar—to the carol service tonight. They're having the final practice now.

JANET. Yes. I've been listening to it. I'd like to come very much, Mr Fawcett.

FAWCETT. Splendid! I told the Vicar you'd enjoy it. And then —(*he hesitates a little*) I suggested you might care to come to the Christmas party we're holding for the old folks afterwards. *Would* you?

JANET. Why—of course.

FAWCETT (*pleased*) Then I'm glad I thought of it. (*He moves to the* R *window*) Mr Worsley's been working terribly hard with the choir—but, of course, he has his problems. Half the boys are tone deaf, you know. And now Mr Felstead—our best alto—has turned Nonconformist.

JANET. Gone over to chapel? How disloyal!

FAWCETT. I never liked him. However—we older ones do our best to make up. (*He moves to* R *of Janet*) Now what about the other ladies—Mrs Prendergast and Miss Goldsworthy? D'you think they'd like to come?

JANET. Oh, I'm sure they would. Miss Goldsworthy's out at the moment, but I think Mrs Prendergast's in her room. (*She rises, puts the Christmas card on the mantelpiece, then moves to the door up* L) I'll go and ask her.

(JANET *exits up* L, *leaving the door open.* FAWCETT *moves up* LC)

(*Off*) Mrs Prendergast, may I come in?

(FAWCETT *rubs his hands, moves to the fireplace, shivers a little, takes another envelope from his pocket, satisfies himself it is the right one, pops it back again, and crosses to* L *of the table.*
JANET *enters up* L, *leaving the door open*)

Yes, Mrs Prendergast is in. She's just coming, and I'm sure Miss Goldsworthy won't be long. She very kindly promised to go to the post-office for me. I'm expecting a parcel, you know. And then she was going to get some fish for her cat.

FAWCETT. Dear little Tabitha. She's devoted to her, isn't she?

JANET. We *all* are, although Mrs Prendergast sometimes pretends she isn't. But we see through her. It makes us smile sometimes.

(RUTH PRENDERGAST *enters up* L. *She is a tall, well-built woman, about five years younger than Janet, and her slightly imperious manner indicates that she has seen better days. She is dressed in an old-fashioned but well-cut dress and wears antique and somewhat bizarre jewellery. She is the widow of a Colonial judge and speaks with an air of quiet authority*)

RUTH. Good afternoon, Mr Fawcett. How are you?
FAWCETT (*crossing below Janet to* R *of Ruth*) Very well, thank you, Mrs Prendergast. (*He shakes hands with Ruth, takes an envelope from his pocket and hands it to her*) The compliments of the season.

(RUTH *extracts the Christmas card from the envelope and glances at it*)

RUTH. How very kind. (*She sits in the armchair*) Ah, you remember my weakness, I see. Look, Janet.
JANET (*moving* L *of Ruth*) Oh, what a fine-looking horse.
RUTH. It's a mare, Janet.
JANET (*vaguely*) Oh—is he? Mr Fawcett's come with an invitation for us, Mrs Prendergast.
RUTH. Really?
FAWCETT (*moving to* R *of Ruth*) Yes—to the carol service—and afterwards to the old people's party.
RUTH. Old people?
FAWCETT. The Vicar wondered whether you could possibly spare time to help with the refreshments, Mrs Prendergast.
RUTH. Help? Oh, I see. I should be delighted.
FAWCETT. Good. The service is at six o'clock and the party begins about seven.
JANET. I'm sure we can manage that.
RUTH. And talking of refreshments, Mr Fawcett, won't you join us in a cup of tea?
FAWCETT. But I mustn't trespass on your time.
RUTH. I've just made some.
JANET. Please do, Mr Fawcett.
FAWCETT. Then how can I refuse?
RUTH. Janet, I wonder if you'd mind . . . ?
JANET. Of course.
RUTH. Thank you, Janet.

(JANET *exits up* L)

Do sit down, Mr Fawcett.
FAWCETT. Thank you. (*He sits* L *of the table*)
RUTH. Janet Bowering's a very charming person—always so anxious to be helpful. We're very fond of her, Miss Goldsworthy and I. She really rather enjoys doing little things for us.

FAWCETT. She was companion to a Lady Glassbury, wasn't she?

RUTH. I believe she was. She misses her very much, I know. But still, here we are, Miss Goldsworthy, Miss Bowering and myself, and we get along with each other very well indeed.

(JANET *enters up* L. *She carries a tray of tea for two which she puts on the table.* FAWCETT *rises*)

JANET. Here's your tea.

RUTH. *Our* tea? Aren't you having any, Janet?

JANET. No, thank you. But let me pour out for you. (*She pours two cups of tea*)

(FAWCETT *moves to the* R *window and looks down at the church*)

FAWCETT. The choir practice is only just over. Mr Worsley's been keeping the younger ones at it very hard. (*He moves to* L *of the table*) He's so anxious for the service to be a success.

RUTH. Naturally.

JANET (*holding out a cup of tea to Fawcett*) Tea?

FAWCETT (*taking the cup from Janet*) Thank you. (*He moves to* R *of the table*)

(JANET *picks up a cup of tea and crosses to* R *of Ruth*)

RUTH. My husband—he was a colonial judge, you know—was very interested in church affairs, especially when we were in the East. (*She takes the cup of tea from Janet*) Thank you. I remember once . . . (*She breaks off*)

(ELEANOR'S *voice is heard off*)

ELEANOR (*off*) Miss Bowering.

JANET (*moving to the door up* L; *frightened*) Yes, Mrs Trellington?

ELEANOR (*off*) Please don't leave your empty milk bottles on the front doorstep. I've asked you so many times.

JANET (*moving up* LC) But I didn't—I . . .

(ELEANOR TRELLINGTON *enters up* L. *She is a woman in her middle forties, obviously fond of clothes, but wearing too many colours and bits and pieces to be well-dressed. She stands* L *of Janet*)

ELEANOR. Why, Mr Fawcett. I beg your pardon, Miss Bowering. I'd no idea . . . How very nice to see you, Mr Fawcett.

FAWCETT (*crossing to* R *of Eleanor*) Good afternoon, Mrs Trellington. (*He shakes hands with her*)

RUTH. That milk bottle was mine. The milk came early this morning and I wasn't fully dressed.

ELEANOR (*playfully*) Ah, so you're the culprit, Mrs Prendergast. (*To Fawcett*) I have to be strict about milk bottles, Mr Fawcett, because poor Miss Goldsworthy had such a nasty fall and cut herself quite badly. Didn't she, Miss Bowering?

ACT I TABITHA

JANET. Oh, yes. Yes.

(ELEANOR *moves to* R *of Ruth and perches on the right arm of her chair.* FAWCETT *moves down* R *and takes a small packet from his pocket*)

ELEANOR (*to Ruth*) So another time, dear, leave the bottle in your room and I'll come and fetch it. It's quite a responsibility, you know, Mr Fawcett, looking after my ladies.

FAWCETT (*crossing below the table to* R *of Eleanor*) But one which you discharge most charmingly, Mrs Trellington. (*He hands her the packet*) And now—with my best wishes.

ELEANOR. What is it? (*She rises*) Oh, no, Mr Fawcett. Not another present, so soon after the other one. (*She opens the package and extracts a brooch*)

FAWCETT. But I insist. I insist. After all—this *is* Christmas time.

(ELEANOR *crosses to the fire and pins the brooch to her dress*)

ELEANOR. I can't accept this. I really can't.

FAWCETT. But you must, please. Not particularly valuable, I'm afraid, but well—like the other little thing I gave you—a bit unusual, eh?

ELEANOR. It's lovely, Mr Fawcett. Thank you so much. By the way, is there any news about Mrs Fenner-Findlay's ring yet?

FAWCETT. None at all, I'm afraid.

JANET (*moving to* R *of Fawcett*) Why? What's happened?

FAWCETT. Oh, didn't you know? About two months ago, Mrs Fenner-Findlay brought in a ring to have a stone reset. (*He crosses to* R *of the table*) And when she called for it a few days later, it had disappeared from the safe.

JANET. Oh, dear.

FAWCETT. It was most mysterious, because the safe was still locked, and I don't see how anyone could have found the place where I hide the key.

ELEANOR. It was a dreadful thing to happen.

FAWCETT. It's been very worrying for me, I can assure you.

RUTH. Was it very valuable?

FAWCETT. Worth about two hundred pounds.

(ELEANOR *moves up* C)

Inspector Bruton and the insurance people are still investigating the matter. Sometimes I think they even suspect me of some kind of fraud.

RUTH. That's absurd, of course.

FAWCETT. All the same, I can see their point of view. But we must try not to worry about it on Christmas Eve.

ELEANOR (*moving to* L *of Janet*) All the same, it's hard not to. It was kind of you to come and see my ladies, Mr Fawcett.

FAWCETT. I've brought an invitation from the Vicar—the carol service—and to the old people's party afterwards.

ELEANOR. How very kind. They'll love it, I'm sure.

(FAWCETT *sits* R *of the table*)

(*To Janet*) Now remember to wrap up well, dear. It's bitterly cold today. Oh, you haven't let your fire out again. You *are* naughty.

JANET. I ran out of shillings.

ELEANOR (*taking a shilling from her purse*) But you only had to ask. Here, let me. (*She crosses to the fireplace and puts a shilling in the meter*) You know, I quite envy you your little outing this evening.

FAWCETT (*half rising*) If *you* could come *too*, Mrs Trellington?

ELEANOR. Me? No—impossible, I'm afraid.

(FAWCETT *resumes his seat*)

(*She takes a box of matches from the mantelpiece and lights the fire*) There's so much to be done here, you know. And Mary will be out, I dare say. Not that I mind that, of course. One mustn't be selfish over young people.

(LAVINIA GOLDSWORTHY *enters quickly up* L *and does not for the moment, see Eleanor.* LAVINIA *is a little, alert old lady of nearly seventy-five, white-haired and rosy-cheeked. She is dressed in outdoor clothes and wears a bright hat. She carries a string bag and a parcel*)

LAVINIA (*crossing to* L *of Janet*) It's all right, Janet.

(FAWCETT *rises*)

I've got your parcel. It was at the post-office. Oh, Mr Fawcett, how do you do?

FAWCETT (*crossing to* R *of Lavinia*) Good afternoon, Miss Goldsworthy. (*He takes an envelope from his pocket and hands it to her*) And a very happy Christmas to you.

LAVINIA. Thank you, Mr Fawcett. What a lovely surprise. (*She takes a Christmas card from the envelope, and exclaims in delight*) Oh, look, Janet. A cat's lovely face.

FAWCETT. Glad you like it. It reminded me of your Tabitha.

LAVINIA. How sweet of you to think of it. (*She puts the card in her string bag*)

(FAWCETT *crosses and resumes his seat* R *of the table*)

(*She hands the parcel to Janet*) Here you are, Janet. (*She notices Eleanor for the first time*) Oh, Mrs Trellington. I didn't see you.

ELEANOR. How kind of you to go to the post-office, Miss Goldsworthy. It's such a long way—in this weather, too. There's a bitter wind.

LAVINIA. But I enjoyed the walk. I quite enjoyed it.

ELEANOR. Well, I'm glad Miss Bowering's parcel has arrived.
LAVINIA. Oh, yes.
ELEANOR. But I really can't understand why you don't have your letters and parcels sent here, Miss Bowering. It would save a lot of trouble—to everyone.

JANET (*putting the parcel on the foot of the bed*) It's just a habit, I suppose. (*She moves down* R) It's silly, but I've always had my things sent poste restante since I was with Lady Glassbury.

(LAVINIA *removes her coat and puts it on the chair* L *of the table*)

We travelled a lot on the Continent, you know, and sometimes changed our hotel at short notice.

ELEANOR. In any case, there was no need for Miss Goldsworthy to go. Mary and I were out shopping this afternoon. We'd have been only too pleased to collect your present. We could have got the cat's fish for you, too.

LAVINIA. Thank you, but I know just the kind of fish Tabitha likes. A most particular cat, my Tabitha, most remarkable.

FAWCETT. A cat of personality, I'm sure.

LAVINIA. Oh, yes. She's not a bit like other cats. For one thing, she doesn't like milk.

FAWCETT. Doesn't like milk?

LAVINIA. No. Isn't it economical of her? When I first took her in—she was a little stray, you know—we put down a saucer of milk for her and she wouldn't touch it. Then we discovered that she liked water. And she insists on her fish being raw. If we cook it, she's most indignant.

RUTH (*rising and crossing to the table*) A cat of low tastes, I'm afraid. (*She refills her cup*) But she's a nice little thing. What did you get for her Christmas dinner, Lavinia?

LAVINIA. Whiting—her favourite.

JANET. Whiting? But doesn't she prefer cod?

RUTH. Oh, no, Janet. It's *always* whiting for special occasions.

LAVINIA. Oh, yes. Whiting. Well, if you'll excuse me, I'll just go and see about her supper.

(FAWCETT *rises*)

(*She crosses to the door up* L.) I shan't be long.

(LAVINIA *exits up* L. RUTH *crosses and sits in the armchair*)

FAWCETT. How she does love that cat. But I can understand it. When my poor Chummy died, it was a terrible blow.

JANET. Chummy was such a dear old dog, wasn't he?

ELEANOR. Yes, yes, he was. He was so friendly, too.

RUTH. I thought I heard you complain that he snapped at you, Mrs Trellington.

ELEANOR. Oh, yes, I believe he did once—but it was only his fun, I'm sure.

FAWCETT. Of course, he was very old—and inclined to be crotchety at times.
JANET. I do hope the poor thing didn't suffer.
FAWCETT. I don't think so. It was quite sudden. I found him lying in the yard. You remember, don't you, Mrs Trellington?
ELEANOR (*moving up* C) Yes—it was just when you were getting over your flu.
JANET (*moving and sitting on the foot of the bed*) Terribly sad.

(LAVINIA *enters up* L. FAWCETT *sits* R *of the table*)

ELEANOR. Well, Miss Goldsworthy, did Tabitha enjoy her supper?
LAVINIA. She hasn't had it yet. She's fast asleep in her basket in my big cupboard.
RUTH. That's very unlike Tabitha.
JANET. She's usually so active.
LAVINIA. Well, I looked in and she didn't stir.
FAWCETT (*leaning confidentially across the table*) Perhaps she was out all night.
LAVINIA. Oh, no, no, no. She's not that sort of cat. She—that is, he—used to be well—quite a Romeo.
RUTH. I should have said more of a Casanova.
LAVINIA. Yes, but he was rather noisy, and Mrs Trellington objected.
ELEANOR. Hardly objected, Miss Goldsworthy. I merely pointed out that something out to be done about it, for everyone's sake.
LAVINIA. Yes, yes. And it was.
ELEANOR. Why, Miss Bowering, you haven't opened your parcel yet.
JANET (*rising*) No, not yet. (*She picks up the parcel and moves down* R)
ELEANOR (*crossing to Janet*) I suppose it's the usual one—the one you get every year, from Lady Glassbury's son?
JANET. It may be.
ELEANOR. Then why don't you open it and find out?
JANET. Well, I thought I'd leave it till the morning. Perhaps Mrs Prendergast will have a present by then.
RUTH. Yes—I was expecting one—from my cousin. It's probably been delayed in the post.
ELEANOR. Personally I can never wait for the right time to open presents—can you, Mr Fawcett?

(LAVINIA *sits above the table*)

FAWCETT. No, no. I can't, either.
ELEANOR. There you are, Miss Bowering.
JANET (*reluctantly*) Very well. Of course—yes. (*She begins to undo the parcel*)

(ELEANOR *hands Janet a knife from the tray*)

Thank you. (*She cuts the string, opens the parcel, and produces a half-bottle of whisky*)

(ELEANOR *moves up* C)

FAWCETT. Why—whisky. What a surprise.
JANET. No—it's not really a surprise at all, Mr Fawcett.
FAWCETT. Indeed! Well, well, Miss Bowering ...
JANET. Oh, it's a joke. Mr Randolph gave me some once, when I had a bad cold. I wasn't used to it and it affected me *most* strangely.
FAWCETT. He must have been *very* distressed about that.
JANET. He wasn't, you know. The next morning he was very witty about it—very witty indeed. And ever since, he's sent me whisky for a Christmas present.
ELEANOR. Last year it was a whole bottle, wasn't it?
JANET. Yes, but this year ...
ELEANOR. Oh well, I suppose everyone's feeling the pinch these days. I know I am.
FAWCETT. I must confess I don't care for whisky.
RUTH. Personally, I'm very *fond* of it. My husband and I always had a peg or two—after sundown, of course.
ELEANOR (*moving to* R *of Ruth*) Then I expect Miss Bowering will give you a peg or two, later—the Christmas spirit, eh?
JANET. Of course.

(*The church clock off strikes the half hour*)

FAWCETT (*jumping up*) Good gracious! Half past five already. I must be off. Oh, Miss Goldsworthy—I nearly forgot. You'll come to the carol service with Mrs Prendergast and Miss Bowering this evening, won't you?
LAVINIA. I should love to.
FAWCETT. Good! Splendid! Good night to you all—and a very merry Christmas.

(ELEANOR *moves up* LC)

(*He moves to* R *of Eleanor*) I suppose you couldn't change your mind about this evening?
ELEANOR. I'm afraid not, Mr Fawcett.
FAWCETT. Oh, well. (*He crosses below Eleanor to the door up* L) Don't bother to show me down. Can find my own way, you know, and I promise not to steal the doormat.

(FAWCETT *exits up* L. ELEANOR *closes the door.* JANET *puts the parcel and the whisky on the bed and sits* R *of the table*)

ELEANOR (*moving* C) So you're all going gay this evening, eh?
LAVINIA. The carols—yes.

ELEANOR. And the party, and the refreshments. You'll enjoy them, won't you?

RUTH. We've been invited to help with the refreshments, Mrs Trellington.

ELEANOR. Yes, yes, I know. And I hope you'll find time for a little tuck-in yourselves.

RUTH. "Tuck-in", Mrs Trellington?

ELEANOR. And why not? Why not take what's going while you can? (*She moves to the door, she stops and turns*) Oh dear, that reminds me. I almost forgot what it was I came to see you about. (*She crosses and sits* L *of the table*) It's the rent, I'm afraid.

JANET. Oh, yes, the rent. (*She rises and moves to the bedside table*) Mine's put away quite safely. It's all ready for you.

LAVINIA. And so is mine.

ELEANOR. It's horrible having to break bad news—on Christmas Eve, too—but it can't be helped.

(JANET *moves to* R *of the table*)

I'm afraid I'll have to put up my rents.

RUTH. What?

JANET. How much?

ELEANOR. I've tried to make it as little as possible. Five shillings a week each, from tomorrow—quarter day.

(JANET *sits* R *of the table*)

LAVINIA. Five shillings. But, Mrs Trellington, I don't think I can.

ELEANOR. Oh dear! That's going to be very awkward, isn't it?

RUTH. I consider any further increase in the charge for our rooms is completely unwarranted.

ELEANOR. I'm sorry you feel that, Mrs Prendergast.

RUTH (*rising*) Not only unwarranted, but disgraceful. I'm not speaking so much for myself as for Miss Goldsworthy and Miss Bowering. They're older than I am, if they'll forgive my saying so, and less fortunately placed financially. (*She moves up* L)

JANET. Mrs Trellington, I've always understood that to raise rents these days—well, it's not legal, is it?

ELEANOR. Legal? Of course it's legal, Miss Bowering. After all I did for you while you were ill—to take that attitude.

JANET. I'm sorry, but as Mrs Prendergast said, Miss Goldsworthy and I find it so difficult to make both ends meet as it is.

ELEANOR. I know. (*She rises*) That's the whole trouble. So do I. (*She crosses down* R) My husband left me this house, so that I should be comfortable after his death. Now it wouldn't be fair to him if I didn't take advantage of it and get all the money I can for these rooms, would it?

LAVINIA. No, no, I suppose not.

ELEANOR. I dare say you'll be able to find an Old People's Home somewhere. They're very comfortable, I believe. Of course, it's not like having a place of your own, but after all . . .
RUTH. Beggars can't be choosers.
ELEANOR. Oh, don't put it like that, Mrs Prendergast.
RUTH (*moving to the fireplace*) How else do you suggest?
JANET. I really don't see . . . Oh, dear. (*She bursts into tears*)

(LAVINIA *rises and moves to* JANET. *There is a knock at the door.*
MARY *enters up* L. *She carries a wrapped bottle of medicine*)

MARY. Conway's have sent your medicine, Miss Bowering. (*She puts the medicine on the chest of drawers, turns and sees* JANET'*s tears*) Why—what's the matter?
LAVINIA. It's about the rent. Mrs Trellington has just told us.
MARY (*puzzled*) The rent? (*She looks enquiringly at Eleanor*)
ELEANOR. Yes, Mary. The fact is . . . Oh, dear, I do feel miserable about this. I've just been telling the ladies I've decided that I shall have to raise the rents of these rooms. There's no other way for me to keep going.
MARY (*moving* C) What?
ELEANOR. And the ladies don't think they'll be able to pay.
LAVINIA. Mary, perhaps if you were to explain . . .
ELEANOR (*cutting in*) There's no need. I quite understand. And I do hope you'll be able to think of something. The increases will start from tomorrow. (*She crosses towards the door up* L)
MARY (*intercepting Eleanor*) You can't do this. You can't. They're paying too much already for these miserable attics.
ELEANOR. Miserable attics? Really!
LAVINIA. Mary, we . . .
MARY. That's all they are. And it isn't as though you needed the money.
ELEANOR. I do need it.
MARY. What for?
ELEANOR. That's my affair.
MARY. And mine, too. You *can't* turn them out, in weather like this—and expect them to trail around looking for somewhere else to live. And you know quite well they won't be able to find anywhere.

(LAVINIA *crosses and sits in the armchair*)

They'd have gone long ago if they could.
ELEANOR. Surely I can do what I like in my own house? This house is mine, you know.

(JANET *rises and crosses to* R *of Lavinia*)

MARY. Oh, yes—I know that.
ELEANOR. You can't think I'm enjoying the prospect of them having to leave, with nowhere to go, can you?

MARY. Yes, I can. You don't care a scrap what happens to them. In fact, you rather enjoy seeing people unhappy.
ELEANOR. Do you really think that?
MARY. I do. You're a hypocrite. And you know it. Towards the end, I think my father knew it, too.
ELEANOR (*suddenly tense; sharply*) Leave your father out of this.
MARY. You never loved him—you only wanted his money.
ELEANOR. How dare you!
MARY. And you got it all right in the end, but it wasn't enough for you. I know what goes on now. Those keys of yours. You've a key for every room and every cupboard. There's nowhere they can hide anything from you. *And* you help yourself sometimes—taking their little things, their presents, even their food—little luxuries they've saved up.
ELEANOR. My dear. I'm afraid you're hysterical, but if that's what you think of me why don't you go? You've no need to stay here if you don't want to.
MARY. If they go, I go, too.
ELEANOR. Very well—you can all go. The whole lot of you. But remember, Mary, you'll find it very different making do on your dispenser's salary. And don't try and raise anything on your father's money, because you can't touch a penny of it, d'you understand? Not one penny. (*She crosses to the door up* L) Well, have a good time at the party.

(ELEANOR *exits up* L)

JANET (*moving up* RC) Oh, my dear.
MARY. I'm sorry that happened in front of you.

(MARY *exits up* L)

JANET (*sitting* L *of the table*) That poor child!
LAVINIA (*rising*) Yes, it was awful for her. And for us, too, to have to hear such things. (*She crosses above the table to* R) I do so hate it when people quarrel, especially when it's about money.
RUTH. Most embarrassing.
JANET. And it doesn't help us, does it? Oh dear, what are we going to do about this rent?
LAVINIA. In my case it doesn't really matter any more.
RUTH. Why not, Lavinia?
LAVINIA. Well, I've come to the end of my tether, as they say. My poor father left me very little, and I've been drawing on it, and now it's all gone.
RUTH (*crossing to* L *of Janet*) But what about your old age pension?
LAVINIA. That's not enough for me to go on living here. I suppose I shall have to go into a home. (*She crosses to the door up* L) I don't think I shall mind really. Some of them are quite nice, I'm told.

(LAVINIA *exits up* L)

JANET. I wish I could be as brave as that. It won't be quite so bad for you, will it?
RUTH (*moving and sitting above the table*) I'm afraid it will.
JANET. But you said just now . . .
RUTH. That was only my stupid pride. I've been selling off things for some time—jewellery and trinkets—and I've very little left. I've even looked about for a cheaper room—but they were all dreadful—even worse than these.
JANET. Then we're all in the same boat?
RUTH. We are—and a very unseaworthy boat, too.

(LAVINIA *enters up* L, *closes the door and leans against it, obviously in distress*)

(*She rises and crosses to Lavinia*) What is it, Lavinia?
LAVINIA. Tabitha! Something terrible—my little Tabitha—she's dead.
RUTH. What?
JANET. Tabitha dead? She can't be.
LAVINIA. Yes, yes. My Tabitha's dead.
RUTH (*leading Lavinia to the armchair*) But, my dear Lavinia, you must be mistaken.

(LAVINIA *sits in the armchair*)

LAVINIA. No, I'm not. Please, please, you go and look at her.

(RUTH *exits up* L)

JANET (*rising and moving to* R *of Lavinia*) Oh, my dear . . .
LAVINIA. She hadn't eaten her fish, so I went to the cupboard. She was still in her basket, asleep I thought. I opened the door wider—and then I saw . . . (*She breaks down*)
JANET. But she hadn't been ill. (*She kneels* R *of Lavinia*) I mean, she was all right before you went out?
LAVINIA. Perfectly. And this morning she was quite gay. She was playing about just as if she were a kitten.

(RUTH *enters up* L. *She carries a small bowl*)

RUTH (*moving up* C) I'm afraid you're right. (*She puts the bowl on the chest of drawers*) Tabitha is dead.
JANET. Oh, dear! What could have been the matter with her?
RUTH. Unless I'm greatly mistaken, she didn't die a natural death.
JANET. You mean the fish?
LAVINIA. But she hadn't even touched the fish.
RUTH. No—it wasn't the fish. I should say it was poison.
JANET (*with a little gasp*) Oh!
RUTH. What is it, Janet?

JANET. Well, a little while ago—you know, when I went to fetch the tea for Mr Fawcett—I was on the landing, and I saw Mrs Trellington come out of Miss Goldsworthy's room.

RUTH (*moving and sitting above the table*) Mrs Trellington?

JANET. I didn't take much notice, because I thought she was just prowling about as usual, seeing what she could find or steal.

RUTH. Did she see you?

JANET. No. She went downstairs. She was smiling to herself.

LAVINIA. You don't think—you don't think Mrs Trellington did it, poisoned my little Tabitha?

RUTH. Well, my dear, what do you think?

LAVINIA. I know she didn't like Tabitha, but I can't believe *anyone* could have poisoned her.

RUTH. But somebody *has*.

LAVINIA. But why *should* she?

(MARY *enters up* L)

MARY (*crossing to* C) Did I hear someone . . . ?

RUTH. Miss Goldsworthy—a terrible shock. Tabitha.

MARY. Tabitha?

RUTH. She's dead.

MARY. No!

RUTH. I'm afraid so.

MARY. How did it happen?

RUTH. We're afraid she's been poisoned.

MARY (*crossing to* L *of Lavinia*) Poisoned?

RUTH. Yes—deliberately.

MARY (*after a slight pause*) This morning, my stepmother was complaining about Tabitha. She'd been disturbed in the night by cats howling. I knew it wasn't Tabitha, and I said so. But she went on about it. Then, later, she said there were rats in the cellar and she wanted some poison. Zinc phosphide, I think it was.

RUTH. Did she get any?

MARY (*after a pause*) Yes—yes, she did. This afternoon. If only I'd realized . . .

LAVINIA. It's not *your* fault, my dear. *You* had nothing to do with it.

MARY. No—I suppose not—not *really*—but . . .

RUTH. *What* did you say the poison was?

MARY (*moving up* C) Zinc phosphide. She said ordinary rat poisons weren't strong enough. She wanted something that would act quickly—more deadly.

RUTH. More deadly? Then she would have had to sign the poison book and give a reason for the purchase?

MARY. Yes. Of course, it may not have been poison that killed Tabitha.

RUTH. In my opinion, it definitely was.

MARY (*moving above the armchair*) Oh, Miss Goldsworthy, I'm so terribly sorry.
LAVINIA. Thank you, dear. I know you are.

(MARY *pauses a moment, then exits up* L)

JANET. My dear, try and be brave. Perhaps, one day, you'll be able to have . . .
LAVINIA. No, I couldn't. Not even if it were possible. My little Tabitha was so sweet—and so trusting. I loved her.
JANET. We all did.
LAVINIA. Yes, I know. But she was mine. It was silly of me to get so fond of her, I suppose, but when you're old and lonely, you must have something to love.
JANET. You're right. Oh, yes, you're right.
RUTH (*indicating the bowl*) This *is* Tabitha's drinking bowl, isn't it?
LAVINIA (*rising*) Yes, I filled it up just before I went out. (*She crosses to* C) The poor little thing didn't drink much of it.
RUTH. No—but she drank enough.
LAVINIA. Enough?
RUTH. This water's been poisoned. There are still some crystals of some sort at the bottom of the bowl.
JANET (*rising*) No! (*She moves up* C *and looks into the bowl*)
LAVINIA. Then it *was* Mrs Trellington.
RUTH. After what Mary told us and Janet saw—there can be no doubt about it.
LAVINIA (*crossing and sitting in the armchair*) But how cruel—how wicked—my poor little cat. (*She breaks down again*)
RUTH. Water, Janet.

(JANET *moves to the bedside table and picks up the jug of water and a tumbler*)

(*She moves to* R *of Lavinia*) Oh, my dear, don't.

(JANET *crosses to Ruth, pours a little water into the glass and hands it to Ruth. Shen then returns to the bedside table, puts the water jug down and notices the whisky on the bed*)

JANET. Mrs Prendergast, what about . . . ?
RUTH. What about what?
JANET (*pointing to the whisky*) This.
RUTH. Whisky. Yes—better still.

(JANET *picks up the whisky and moves to* RUTH, *who pours some whisky into the glass of water*)

Here we are. (*She holds out the glass to Lavinia*) Just what you need. Drink this, my dear Lavinia.
LAVINIA (*trying to compose herself*) What is it?
RUTH. A little whisky. It will do you good.

LAVINIA. Oh! (*She drinks and coughs*)
RUTH. Now come along.
LAVINIA. It's very strong, isn't it?
RUTH. Only because you're not used to it. I only gave you a little.
JANET. Mrs Prendergast—I wonder—would you care for a little, too?
RUTH. Well, it might do us *all* good, after this very nasty shock. I will, if you will.
JANET. I—I don't think I will, you know.
RUTH. Nonsense! Fetch some glasses, Janet.
JANET. Very well. (*She fetches two glasses from the cupboard* L) I suppose we might as well have some while we can.
RUTH. Of course. Before Mrs Trellington drinks the lot. Shall I pour?
JANET. Yes, please do.

(RUTH *pours some whisky into the glasses*)

Oh, not too much for me.
RUTH (*handing a glass to Janet*) Do you good. How are you feeling, Lavinia?
LAVINIA. I think I'm feeling better, thank you.
RUTH. I thought you would be. (*She drinks*) A very good whisky this.
JANET. And very refreshing, too. (*She sips, then sits* L *of the table*) I suppose—no—I suppose it couldn't be proved.
RUTH (*moving and sitting above the table*) What couldn't be proved, Janet? (*She puts the bottle on the table*)
JANET. That Mrs Trellington poisoned Tabitha.
RUTH. If a human being had been murdered, it would be proved all right.
JANET. But then, of course, Tabitha *wasn't* a human being—and to kill a cat isn't murder.
RUTH. Why not? Hasn't an animal the same right to live?
LAVINIA. Yes—yes, of course he has.
RUTH. In the East, I can assure you that *all* life is sacred. (*She takes another drink, rises and speaks a little louder*) Killing Tabitha, out of sheer malice, is just as much murder as if a man or woman had been destroyed.
JANET. But not in the eyes of the law.
RUTH. Never mind about the law. (*She drinks*)

(JANET *tops up Ruth's glass*)

(*She sweeps on with her argument*) Mrs Trellington has shown herself to be evil all through.
LAVINIA. It's a dreadful thing to say, but I think she is.
JANET. I think Mary was right when she said Mrs Trellington enjoyed seeing people unhappy.

RUTH. And whenever she sees happiness, she sets out to destroy it. (*She drinks*) That was good whisky.
JANET. Do have another one?
RUTH (*rising and moving* L *of Janet*) No, thank you, Janet. Well—perhaps.

(JANET *pours some more whisky for Ruth*)

Tell me, why should we allow her to go on like this?
LAVINIA. Because we've no way of stopping her.
RUTH. On the contrary—we have. What are you going to do with the rest of this whisky, Janet?
JANET. Hide it away in my cupboard, I suppose. Then—if there's any left—we might have a little tomorrow.
RUTH. If there's any *left*. But you know quite well what will happen. While we're out, Mrs Trellington will help herself. However carefully you lock it up and hide it, she'll manage to get at it.
JANET. Yes—I'm afraid so.

(RUTH *takes another drink.* JANET *and* LAVINIA *watch, fascinated*)

RUTH (*crossing to the fireplace*) Now listen to me, both of you. Tabitha was poisoned, wasn't she?
LAVINIA. Yes.
RUTH. And that poison was put into Tabitha's drinking water, wasn't it?
LAVINIA. Yes, it was.
RUTH. Suppose we poured some of that water into the whisky before Janet hides it.
JANET. Mrs Prendergast!
RUTH. You'd re-cork the bottle and lock it up in your cupboard—where, presumably, it should be safe from Mrs Trellington or any other petty thief.
JANET. But—if Mrs Trellington drank it—it would be murder.
RUTH (*crossing to* L *of Janet*) Why? It's your whisky, isn't it? Haven't you a right to do what you like with it? If you choose to pour water into it—water from a cat's drinking bowl—it's entirely your own affair.
LAVINIA. But *we* know it's poisoned—and if you leave it about for someone to take . . .
RUTH. But Janet won't be leaving it about. She's going to lock it up in her cupboard. She's doing everything humanly possible to *prevent* anyone taking it.
JANET. But—suppose Mrs Trellington *did* drink it?
RUTH (*taking another drink*) That would be her funeral. I should consider it just retribution. (*She drinks*)
JANET. No—no—we couldn't. (*She sips her drink*) Supposing we were found out?
RUTH (*moving and sitting above the table*) We couldn't be found

out. If Mrs Trellington were to drink that whisky and die, what would be the evidence in a coroner's court? She bought the poison, gave a false reason for doing so, and signed the poison book. There could be only one of two verdicts—suicide or accident. (*To Lavinia*) What do *you* say, Lavinia?

LAVINIA (*clutching her glass*) I hate her—of *course* I hate her. (*She rises and moves* C) I suppose I shouldn't. I've been brought up to love my enemies—to forgive them.

RUTH. Can you forgive the death of Tabitha?

LAVINIA (*looking bewildered and distressed*) No—no—no. But we've no right to take the law into our own hands.

RUTH. But we're not. We're merely creating a situation where she takes the law—or a disregard for the law—into her own.

LAVINIA (*moving and sitting* R *of the table*) But I know it's wrong.

RUTH. Remember, we're giving the woman a chance.

LAVINIA. You mean—if she *doesn't* steal the whisky . . . ?

RUTH. Yes. She didn't give your Tabitha a chance, did she? And, as you say, if she *doesn't* steal the whisky, no harm will come to her.

LAVINIA. Very well. Yes. Very well.

JANET (*very frightened*) Miss Goldsworthy!

LAVINIA (*nearly as excited as Ruth; wildly*) She killed Tabitha. The only thing that loved me. She killed her cruelly. And she should be punished for it.

JANET. Yes, but not like . . .

RUTH. If you'd rather not have anything to do with this, Janet . . .

JANET. Oh, no. I agree. But . . .

RUTH (*quickly*) You agree. Good! (*She rises, gets the drinking bowl and tries to pour the poisoned water into the bottle of whisky*) I'm going to spill this, you know. Funny! I thought I had quite a steady hand.

LAVINIA. Better pour it into the jug first.

RUTH (*collecting the jug from the bedside table*) Good idea. (*She pours the water from the bowl into the jug, then starts to fill up the bottle from the jug*)

(MARY *enters quickly up* L)

MARY. There's something I want to tell you . . . (*She stops in astonishment as she sees the whisky bottle and jug in Ruth's hands*) What on earth . . . ?

(RUTH *sits above the table*)

RUTH (*the first to recover; rather lamely*) Hallo, Mary. We are having a little drink—and we found it rather strong.

MARY. Then you'd better take more water with it.

RUTH. That's what we thought.

MARY. Now, listen. I came to tell you that . . .

ELEANOR (*off*) Mary—there's somebody at the door—and I'm changing. Answer it, please.
MARY. While I was out shopping this afternoon . . .
ELEANOR (*off*) Mary! Didn't you hear me?
MARY (*calling*) Yes. All right. (*To the others*) I'll be back later.

(MARY *exits up* L)

LAVINIA. Do you think she noticed anything?
RUTH. No—I shouldn't think so. (*She resumes her pouring*) Now, Janet, watch!
JANET. Stop!
RUTH (*looking at the bottle*) That'll do. (*She puts down the jug and corks the bottle, then rises, hands the bottle to Janet and replaces the water jug on the bedside table*) Lock it away in your cupboard, Janet.

(JANET *rises, moves to the small cupboard above the bed and puts the bottle in it*)

Put it at the back—behind those tins. Then there can be no question of her drinking it accidentally, can there?

(JANET *closes the cupboard and locks it*)

(*She tries the cupboard to make sure it is firmly secured*) That's the only key—so far as you know?

(JANET *nods*)

Then put it away safely in your handbag.

(JANET *moves to the chest of drawers and puts her key in her handbag*)

(*She carefully watches Janet*) That's right.

(*The church clock off strikes the three-quarters*)

Now we must get ready for the carol service. (*She moves to the table, collects the tea-things on to the tray, and moves to the door up* L)
LAVINIA. Yes. Very well. (*She rises*) I'll put my things on. (*She crosses and opens the door for Ruth*)

(RUTH *exits up* L. LAVINIA *closes the door and looks at Janet.*
JANET *moves to the table, picks up the glasses and exits to the scullery.* LAVINIA *collects the bowl and moves towards the door up* L.
JANET *re-enters from the scullery*)

JANET (*as she enters*) We can't do it—we *can't*, you know.

(LAVINIA *stops and turns*)

I don't care what Mrs Prendergast says—it's murder. That's what it is—*murder*.
LAVINIA. Only if she *does* steal the whisky.

JANET. She *will*. I know she will—and so do you, Miss Goldsworthy. It'll be murder. Even if we're not found out, it will still be murder.

LAVINIA (*thinking clearly at last; calmly*) Yes. You're right. (*She crosses and sits above the table*)

JANET (*sitting R of the table; distressed*) Oh, *why* did we agree?

LAVINIA. I must have been beside myself for the moment. The whisky, perhaps. Poor Tabitha—and—Mrs Prendergast—she's so convincing—so *forceful*.

JANET. We must *do* something. We can't go on with it.

LAVINIA. We must pour the whisky away.

JANET. Mrs Prendergast will be very angry with us—after we agreed.

LAVINIA. I know. I'm sorry about that—but all the same . . .

JANET (*as a thought strikes her*) Wait! I think I see what we can do—so that Mrs Prendergast doesn't find out.

LAVINIA. What's that, Janet?

JANET. You remember when I opened my parcel—when Mrs Trellington was here?

(LAVINIA *nods*)

She said something about there being only a half bottle this year. Well, there was another one in the parcel—(*she rises and moves to the bed*) another half bottle. Mrs Trellington didn't see it, because of all the packing. (*She takes a second half bottle of whisky from the parcel*) Here it is. (*She moves to R of Lavinia and hands her the bottle*)

LAVINIA. Oh, Janet! (*She breaks the seal*)

JANET. Now we'll pour the poisoned whisky down the sink and put this one—(*she indicates the bottle in Lavinia's hand*) in its place. (*She moves up C and takes the cupboard key from her handbag*) Then, if Mrs Trellington does drink it, nothing will happen. (*She moves to the cupboard above the bed, unlocks it and takes out the bottle of poisoned whisky*)

LAVINIA. And Mrs Prendergast?

JANET. She won't know we've changed the bottles. (*She hands the poisoned bottle to Lavinia*) She'll just think she was wrong about the water in Tabitha's bowl having been poisoned.

LAVINIA (*with heartfelt relief*) Oh, Janet! What a good idea. (*She puts the bottles on the table*)

JANET. That's the solution, isn't it?

LAVINIA. Yes—of course it is.

JANET (*picking up the poisoned bottle*) We haven't much time.

(JANET *exits with the poisoned bottle to the scullery*. LAVINIA *rises.* JANET *re-enters with an empty bottle*)

LAVINIA. Under the pillow.

(JANET *puts the empty bottle under the pillow on her bed.* LAVINIA *picks up the good bottle and hands it to* JANET, *who puts it in the cupboard above the bed, locks the cupboard, and puts the key in her handbag.* LAVINIA *tidies the bed.*

RUTH *enters up* L, *leaving the door open. She wears outdoor clothes*)

RUTH. Aren't you ready yet?

LAVINIA. I'll get my things at once.

(LAVINIA *picks up the bowl, collects her coat and exits up* L)

RUTH. What have you two been doing all this time?

JANET (*moving to the cupboard* L) Well, I cleared away the glasses and tidied up . . .

RUTH. Well, put on your warmest things.

JANET (*taking her coat from the cupboard*) Yes—I will. (*She puts on her coat*)

RUTH. And a scarf for your head.

JANET. Yes—I've got one in my pocket. (*She takes her scarf and gloves from her coat pockets*)

(LAVINIA *puts her head round the door up* L)

LAVINIA. I'm quite ready now.

RUTH. Good. (*She crosses to the door up* L) Let's go. I'm going to enjoy this party.

LAVINIA *withdraws her head.*

RUTH *exits up* L. JANET *moves to the fireplace and turns out the gas fire as—*

the CURTAIN *falls*

ACT II

SCENE—*The same. Nine p.m. the same evening.*

When the CURTAIN *rises, the room is just as it was at the end of the previous Act, except that the lights and the gas fire have been turned off. From the Causeway comes the sound of a band of carol singers, led by a cornet player, amateurish but not unpleasant. After a few moments,* JANET *and* LAVINIA *enter up* L, *dressed as they were when we last saw them.* JANET *switches on the lights, crosses to the table and puts her handbag on it.* LAVINIA *moves up* C.

JANET. How cold it always is in this room.
LAVINIA. It might be better if you pulled the curtains.
JANET (*looking out of the* R *window*) But I like to see the lights from the church. (*She looks down*) Why, there's Mr Fawcett and his waits off carol-singing again. He really oughtn't to be out in the streets on a night like this.
LAVINIA (*removing her coat, hat and scarf*) But he does enjoy it so. D'you remember how he always used to walk round the park with Chummy every morning? He must miss him terribly.
JANET (*moving to* R *of Lavinia*) Yes. It was a lovely party, wasn't it? (*She takes Lavinia's clothes and puts them in the cupboard up* L)
LAVINIA. Yes, it was. (*She pauses*) Tabitha always slept at night under my counterpane.
JANET. Would you like to move your bed in here?
LAVINIA. No, thank you. I must make up my mind to get used to it. Mrs Trellington would be certain to object.
JANET. If Mrs Trellington insists on this rent increase, it won't matter what she thinks much longer. (*She removes her coat, scarf and gloves and puts them in the cupboard up* L)
LAVINIA. The rent! Oh, dear me, yes.
JANET. I still don't understand. We've tried to be good tenants. We've never done her any harm. I suppose Mrs Prendergast is right. Mrs Trellington is just an evil woman.
LAVINIA. She must be. I know my Tabitha never did her any harm. It almost makes me wish . . .
JANET (*moving to the fireplace*) I'll light the fire. (*She takes the matches from the mantelpiece, kneels and lights the gas fire*) D'you think Mrs Prendergast will be long?
LAVINIA. I don't know. Mr Sandford asked her to stay on for a few minutes and meet some people from Hong Kong.
JANET (*rising and looking towards the cupboard above the bed*) I wonder if—if Mrs Trellington has . . . ?

LAVINIA (*looking towards the cupboard*) Do you think we'd better find out before Mrs Prendergast gets back?

JANET (*crossing to the table*) Yes—I think we'd better. (*She takes her key from her handbag, moves to the cupboard above the bed, unlocks it and takes out the bottle of whisky. Nearly a quarter of it has gone*) Look, some of it's gone. (*She moves to* R *of the table*)

LAVINIA. So she did steal it. Mrs Prendergast was right. (*She sits* L *of the table*) Thank goodness we changed the bottles. If we hadn't ...

JANET. I don't know how we're going to explain to Mrs Prendergast. Oh, dear. (*She moves to the cupboard, replaces the bottle, locks the cupboard and keeps the key*) Would you like a cup of tea?

LAVINIA. No, thank you, my dear.

(RUTH *enters up* L)

RUTH (*moving* C) I got away as soon as I could. Well?

JANET (*moving to* R *of Ruth*) It was all very pleasant, wasn't it? The singing and the party?

RUTH. Never mind about the party. Has anything happened? Mrs Trellington? The whisky?

JANET } (*together*) { Oh, yes. The whisky. She didn't touch it.
LAVINIA }   { Yes, she did.

RUTH. Did she or didn't she?

JANET. No.

RUTH. She *didn't?*

JANET. I mean, I don't think so—I ...

RUTH. Have you looked?

JANET. Yes.

RUTH. And it hasn't been touched?

JANET (*very nervously*) No—no.

RUTH. Let me see for myself, Janet.

JANET. Really—I ... (*She looks despairingly at Lavinia, moves to the cupboard above the bed, unlocks it and takes out the bottle*)

RUTH (*moving to Janet and taking the bottle from her*) But she *has* taken some. Nearly a quarter of it's gone.

JANET. Yes, yes. I suppose it has.

RUTH (*returning the bottle to Janet*) Then I wonder how she's feeling?

(JANET *puts the bottle on the chest of drawers*)

(*She moves down* L) But, Janet, why did you say she hadn't touched it?

JANET. Well, you see, I thought, and Miss Goldsworthy thought, too ...

LAVINIA. Yes, yes. I did. Janet was right. Mrs Trellington didn't take any of that whisky.

RUTH. You don't mean someone else took it?

JANET. Oh, no. It was Mrs Trellington all right ...

RUTH. Oh, dear! What *have* I done? She may be ill—dying—even dead. But it's too late now.

LAVINIA. No, it isn't too late.

RUTH (*sitting in the armchair*) It is, if she drank that whisky.

LAVINIA. She didn't. Nobody drank it. We threw it away. Janet and I changed the bottles.

RUTH. What?

JANET. You see, there were two half-bottles of whisky in my parcel. I hid the second one while I was undoing the parcel, because Mrs Trellington was here watching.

LAVINIA. And just before we went to the party, Janet and I changed our minds. Didn't we?

JANET. Yes. We threw the poisoned whisky away down the sink and put the new bottle in the cupboard instead. Look—(*she moves to the head of the bed and takes the empty bottle from under the pillow*) this is the bottle which had the poisoned whisky.

RUTH (*rising and moving* C) You mean, the whisky Mrs Trellington stole was harmless?

LAVINIA. Yes.

JANET. Quite harmless. (*She replaces the empty bottle under the pillow*)

RUTH (*moving* LC; *with a sigh of relief*) Well, thank heavens you came to your senses before I did. (*She sits in the armchair*) How I ever came to think of such a thing . . .

LAVINIA. But you didn't want it to happen when you saw clearly, did you? (*She rises and moves to* R *of Ruth*) Look at it this way. Why did you change your mind? Was it only because you were afraid we might be found out?

RUTH. Maybe.

LAVINIA. But you repented?

RUTH. You might call it that, perhaps. Does it make any difference?

LAVINIA. Of course. My dear father used to say that if you were really sorry, your sins would be wiped away, just as if they had never been committed.

RUTH. It sounds very easy, doesn't it?

LAVINIA (*moving to* L *of the table and sitting; slightly offended*) My father was a very good man, and I'm sure he knew best.

JANET. Wouldn't it be better to try and put the whole thing out of our minds and think about something else? (*She sits above the table*) It's Christmas Eve, you know, and tomorrow will be Christmas Day. Oh, dear!

LAVINIA. Yes?

JANET. Christmas Day—quarter day, too. This increase in rent.

LAVINIA. We must trust in God.

JANET. You mean, perhaps Mr Sandford or the Church might help us?

RUTH. No! That would be charity.

LAVINIA. Yes, I know. But there's nothing wrong in charity, is there? If everyone were too proud to accept charity, nobody would be able to bestow it, and then they wouldn't be rewarded for their good deeds, would they?

RUTH (*rising and removing her hat and coat*) Charity means the sacrifice of one's independence. (*She puts her hat and coat on the chair down* L)

LAVINIA. I'm afraid I've never been a very independent person. And now that Tabitha's gone, I don't really mind the idea of going into a home. At least, not so much.

(RUTH *sits in the armchair*)

JANET. Perhaps something will turn up. I remember Lady Glassbury saying that when we were in Monte Carlo one winter. She'd had a very unpleasant letter from her bank manager, and, do you know—she went to the Casino that night, put a hundred francs on a single number, and it *won*. Wouldn't it be wonderful if something like that happened to us?

(*There is a knock on the door*)

(*She calls*) Come in.

(MARY *enters up* L *and moves* C)

(*Relieved*) Oh, it's you, my dear. I was afraid . . .

MARY. My stepmother's gone out.

RUTH. Gone out?

MARY. Yes.

JANET. By herself?

MARY. Yes.

LAVINIA. Walking?

MARY. Yes, it's all right. I just knocked on her door and there was no reply. (*She crosses to Janet*) Miss Bowering, this arrived for you while you were at the carol service. (*She hands Janet an envelope*) Miss Burrington left it. It looks like another Christmas card.

JANET. How thoughtful of her—and I'm afraid I didn't send her one this year. (*She opens the envelope*)

MARY (*moving to* R *of Ruth*) Was the party fun?

LAVINIA. Yes, it was splendid. Everyone was most kind, and the refreshments were excellent.

MARY. Good.

RUTH. Personally, I thought some of the old folks were extremely greedy.

LAVINIA. I dare say they were hungry, poor things.

JANET. I know I was. (*She displays the card*) Mary, do look at this.

(MARY *moves to* L *of Janet*)

Isn't it a lovely card?

MARY. Lovely.

JANET (*rising and crossing to* R *of Ruth*) And so seasonable, too. (*She shows the card to Ruth*) A picture of an enormous roast turkey.

RUTH. It looks most appetising.

(JANET *crosses to the fireplace and puts the card on the mantelpiece*)

MARY (*sitting above the table*) While we're on our own, there's something I'd like to say to you.

RUTH. Yes, of course.

MARY. It's about your rents. I do wish I could do something, but, as you know, I can't. You heard, didn't you? My stepmother has control of everything.

RUTH. What a pity your father made such an unfortunate will.

MARY (*grimly*) I don't think he had much choice.

JANET. And you can't do anything?

MARY. Not as things are—no.

RUTH. But surely you get some of the income from his property?

MARY. No—nothing at all—during my stepmother's lifetime.

LAVINIA. Then I'm very glad you've got your job at the hospital, my dear, so that you can leave here whenever you want to. Otherwise the same thing might happen to you as it did to me. I stayed at home too long—looking after my father. Then, when he died, it was too late—too late to begin a new life. I was getting old myself. Otherwise, I might have married—had children. It may sound ridiculous now, but they said I was quite pretty once.

MARY (*rising*) I'm sure you were.

LAVINIA. But not as pretty as you, my dear. In fact, I'm surprised you're not married already. I think the young men in this city are being very slow.

MARY (*laughing and crossing to the door up* L) Do you?

(MARY *exits up* L)

LAVINIA. Dear Mary.

JANET (*crossing to* R *of Ruth*) Now do let me make a cup of tea for us all. You will have some, won't you?

RUTH. Well, perhaps I will.

JANET (*crossing to* R) I'm so glad. I'll put the kettle on.

(JANET *exits to the scullery*)

LAVINIA. I'd no idea Mary had been left in such a difficult position, had you?

RUTH. No, poor girl.

LAVINIA. It certainly looks as though she had even more to put up with than we knew. My dear father . . .

(*The sound of running footsteps is heard off up* L)

MARY (*off*) Mrs Prendergast!

(MARY *bursts into the room, very distressed.*
JANET *enters from the scullery*)

(*She runs* C) Mrs Prendergast!
RUTH (*rising and moving to Mary*) What is it, Mary?
MARY. My stepmother.
RUTH. What's happened?
MARY. She's dead.
RUTH. My dear . . .
MARY. She is, I tell you. She's dead.

(*The others glance guiltily at each other.* LAVINIA *rises.* RUTH *puts Mary in the armchair*)

RUTH. Pro—probably she's only fainted.

(RUTH *exits up* L)

MARY. I thought she'd gone out. I told you. But when I went to her room a moment ago, I found her lying on the bed. She must have been there the first time I knocked.
JANET (*guiltily*) My dear! How dreadful. It must have been a stroke of some sort.
LAVINIA (*guiltily*) Or her heart? (*She sits on the right arm of Mary's chair*) Did she suffer from her heart?
MARY. Not that I know of. I never remember her being ill—never. She was perfectly all right when I last saw her—just before you went out.
LAVINIA (*rising; startled*) Just before we went out?
JANET. No—it couldn't have been that.
MARY. It couldn't have been what?
LAVINIA. Nothing, my dear—nothing. At least, nothing that could possibly have any bearing on what's happened.

(RUTH *enters up* L *and moves to the fireplace. She looks very grave*)

MARY. She *is* dead? Oh, how awful!

(*The front-door bell rings off*)

JANET. That's the front door.
LAVINIA. I'll see who it is.

(LAVINIA *collects her coat and exits up* L)

MARY. I feel dreadful about this, after what happened this evening—all those awful things I said to her.
RUTH. That doesn't alter the fact that they were true.
MARY. I know, but . . .
RUTH. There's no point in ascribing non-existent virtues to people, just because they're dead.

(FAWCETT *enters up* L *and crosses to* C.
LAVINIA *follows him on*)

FAWCETT. What's all this?
RUTH. Hasn't Miss Goldsworthy told you?
FAWCETT. Mrs Trellington? Yes. But how did it happen?
LAVINIA. We don't know.
FAWCETT. I was on my way home, and I just popped in to see how you enjoyed the carols and the party. But when did you find out about this dreadful thing?
LAVINIA. Poor Mary went to her stepmother's room . . .
MARY. I was going to light her gas fire.
LAVINIA. And found her there, lying on the bed.
FAWCETT. Poor girl. What an awful shock for you—for us all. We must get a doctor—at once. Doctor Greenslade's away for Christmas, but young Brentwood's on duty, isn't he? I'll go and fetch him.
MARY. Thank you, Mr Fawcett.

(FAWCETT *exits up* L. MARY *rises and looks at Ruth*)

RUTH. Yes, dear?
MARY. I think I'd like to go to my room for a little while.
RUTH. I'll come with you.

(MARY *exits up* L.
RUTH *follows her off*)

LAVINIA. Poor thing. (*She crosses to* C) I suppose we ought to feel sad, too, but somehow I don't, you know.
JANET. Miss Goldsworthy!
LAVINIA. But Mary will own this house now—and there'll be no increase in rent. You see what I mean?
JANET. Yes, I do—but all the same . . .
LAVINIA. Isn't it funny—only a few minutes ago, we were saying something might happen.
JANET. And it has.

(RUTH *enters up* L *and moves to* L *of Lavinia*)

LAVINIA. Well—what do you think?
RUTH. I don't know what to think.
LAVINIA (*rather disappointed*) Perhaps she *has* only fainted.
RUTH. No—she's dead. There's no doubt about that, Lavinia.
JANET. Then I'm sure I was right. It must have been a stroke.
LAVINIA. But such a strange coincidence, isn't it?
RUTH. I think the least said, the better. (*She sits in the armchair*) There's no telling what's happened, till the doctor's been.
LAVINIA. I do wish he'd hurry.
JANET. He won't be a moment. He lives only just round the corner.
LAVINIA (*moving to* R *of Ruth*) Of course, as I was just saying to Janet—there won't be any increase in rent *now*.

(*The front door slams off*)

FAWCETT (*off; calling*) It's all right. Only us.
JANET (*sitting* R *of the table*) Then the doctor was at home. That's good.
LAVINIA. I dare say he'll be able to do something.
RUTH (*tensely*) Do be quiet, Lavinia.

(LAVINIA *moves above the table.*
FAWCETT *enters up* L *and moves* C)

FAWCETT. I told the doctor you were all here and he's coming up directly he's examined the . . .
RUTH. Body?
FAWCETT. Yes, yes. Well, well, well! What a terrible thing to happen—on Christmas Eve, too. Miss Trellington not here?
RUTH. She's gone to her room.
FAWCETT. Yes, of course. It's terrible—terrible. Only a few hours ago we were all in this room—happy and joking.
RUTH. Yes.
FAWCETT. So unselfish, wasn't she? Even too busy to come to the carol service. Preparing for tomorrow's festivities, I suppose.
LAVINIA (*looking very embarrassed*) Perhaps she was.
FAWCETT. Never a thought for herself.

(*There is a tap at the door.*
MARTIN *enters up* L)

Here we are, Doctor. Here we are.
MARTIN. Good evening.

(FAWCETT *crosses to the door and closes it*)

RUTH. Well, Doctor?
MARTIN (*moving* C) I'm afraid there's nothing to be done.
RUTH. A heart attack, or some sort of seizure, I suppose?
MARTIN. There's no telephone in this house, is there?
RUTH. No, Doctor.
MARTIN (*moving to* R *of Fawcett*) I wonder if you'd mind making a call for me, Mr Fawcett?
FAWCETT. Of course, Doctor.
MARTIN. I want you to get through to the police station . . .

(*The Old Ladies react*)

LAVINIA (*sitting above the table*) The police station!
MARTIN (*with a glance at Lavinia*) Yes. (*To Fawcett*) Ask them to send someone along as soon as possible.
FAWCETT (*breathlessly*) I will, Doctor.
MARTIN. Say you're speaking on my behalf, will you? And that it's urgent. Say that Mrs Trellington has died suddenly and that, quite frankly, I'm not prepared to sign the death certificate.

FAWCETT. Yes, of course.

(FAWCETT *exits up* L, *closing the door behind him.* MARTIN *moves to the fireplace*)

RUTH. Dr Brentwood, is it necessary to involve the police?
MARTIN. Unfortunately, yes.
LAVINIA. But if Mrs Trellington died of a stroke or a heart attack . . .
MARTIN. She didn't, Miss Goldsworthy. This is going to be a great shock to you, I'm afraid. There are signs that Mrs Trellington has been poisoned.
JANET. Poisoned?

(RUTH *rises and moves up* C)

MARTIN. Naturally I can't give a definite opinion yet, but all the symptoms point to poison.
LAVINIA. But that's impossible. She couldn't have been poisoned, I'm sure.
MARTIN. What makes you say that?
LAVINIA. Because, well . . .

(RUTH *restrains Lavinia by placing a hand on her shoulder and crossing to* R *of her*)

Well, how could she?
RUTH. You mean that she committed suicide?
MARTIN. Perhaps. There are other possibilities, too.
RUTH. But if there were signs of poison, she must have taken it herself.
MARTIN. Why, Mrs Prendergast? Have you ever heard her threaten to take her life?
RUTH. No.
MARTIN. Mr Fawcett said that Mary was up here with you.
RUTH. She was. I took her to her room. Do you want to see her?
MARTIN. Yes, I think I'd better. Would you mind fetching her?
RUTH. Certainly, Doctor. (*She starts to go, then decides that it would be unwise to leave Martin alone with Janet and Lavinia, and stops up* LC) Janet, you go.
JANET (*rising*) Yes, certainly.

(JANET *crosses and exits up* L)

RUTH (*sitting in the armchair*) But, Doctor, people who take their own lives don't always announce it in advance, do they?
MARTIN. I agree. Sometimes the impulse is quite sudden. But one can usually find a reason, of course.

(MARY *enters up* L *and moves* C.
JANET *follows her on and stands up* C)

(*He crosses to* L *of Mary*) Why, Mary—I'm terribly sorry about this.
MARY. I'm glad you were able to come so quickly.
MARTIN. You've told her, Miss Bowering?
JANET (*crossing to* R *of the table*) Yes. (*She sits* R *of the table*)
MARY. That you've sent for the police? Yes.
MARTIN. I'm afraid I had no alternative. You see, Mary, it looks to me as though your stepmother's been poisoned.
MARY. Poisoned?
RUTH. The doctor thinks she may have committed suicide.
MARTIN. Oh, no, Mrs Prendergast. I only said it was a possibility. Mary, darling, when the police come, they're bound to ask a lot of questions, so I thought I'd better prepare you a little.
MARY. I just can't understand it, Martin.
MARTIN. You've never heard her threaten to do away with herself?
MARY. No.
MARTIN. Was she in trouble of any sort—financial difficulties?
MARY. None that I knew of.
MARTIN. In fact, you can't think of any reason at all?
MARY. No, I can't.
MARTIN. Well, darling, suppose it was an accident. Had she any poison in her possession?
LAVINIA. Yes, she had.
MARTIN. What?
LAVINIA. She bought some poison—only this afternoon.
MARTIN (*crossing to* L *of Lavinia*) How do you know that, Miss Goldsworthy?
LAVINIA. Because Mary told us, this evening.
MARTIN (*to Mary*) Your stepmother bought some poison this afternoon?
MARY. No. I did.
LAVINIA. *You* did?
RUTH. But, Mary, you gave us to understand that your stepmother bought it, and signed the poison book.
MARY (*moving up* LC) Yes, I know—and I'm terribly sorry.
MARTIN. What was it?
MARY. Zinc phosphide.
MARTIN. And you signed for it?
MARY. Yes—at Conway's.
MARTIN. And yet you told the ladies that your stepmother had bought it? (*He moves to* R *of Mary*)
MARY. It's quite simple. We went shopping this afternoon, but it was getting rather late, so she came home and left me to finish. She gave me the shopping list and told me to go to Conway's to get some zinc phosphide. It was on the list. I asked her why she wanted it. She said it was to kill rats.
MARTIN. What did you do with the stuff?

MARY. I put it in my shopping basket and brought it back with the rest of the things.

MARTIN. You didn't buy any other drugs at Conway's, I suppose? Anything that could have been mistaken for . . .

MARY. No.

MARTIN. And that's all you know about it?

MARY (*crossing down* RC) Yes.

MARTIN (*after a pause*) But I still don't understand why you said it was your stepmother who bought the poison.

MARY (*turning to Martin*) I didn't say that—not really. But, you see, after Miss Goldsworthy found Tabitha dead——

MARTIN (*moving* C) Tabitha dead?

MARY. —I realized why she'd wanted the poison. So I let Miss Goldsworthy assume that *she'd* bought it. (*She moves to* R *of Lavinia*) I did come up to explain, as a matter of fact, but poor Miss Goldsworthy was so terribly upset, I couldn't bear to let her think I'd had any part in it, even unintentionally.

(FAWCETT *enters up* L)

FAWCETT. They're here, Doctor. Detective Inspector Bruton, the surgeon and a police sergeant. They're downstairs.

MARTIN. Right.

(MARTIN *crosses and exits up* L)

FAWCETT (*moving* C) Oh, dear, this is dreadful. A terrible business. Why has Dr Brentwood brought in the police?

RUTH. He has some idea that Mrs Trellington was poisoned.

FAWCETT. I can't believe it! Dear me, I really feel most upset. If there's nothing more I can do, I think I'll be getting along home. (*He moves to the door up* L)

MARY (*crossing to Fawcett*) Thank you, Mr Fawcett, for all you've done.

FAWCETT. Not at all. It's been a pleasure. I mean, I'm only too glad to help.

(FAWCETT *exits up* L, *closing the door behind him*)

MARY (*crossing and sitting* L *of the table*) May I stay with you for a while?

JANET. Yes, my dear—of course.

(MARTIN *enters up* L *and moves* C)

MARTIN. I'm sorry to say that the police surgeon confirms what I thought—poison. The police have taken charge.

LAVINIA. Oh, dear!

MARTIN. Tell me, Mary, was your stepmother in the habit of taking spirits?

MARY. When she could get them—yes. Why?

MARTIN. We've just found a glass of whisky by her bed.

RUTH (*shocked*) Whisky!
LAVINIA. Did you say *whisky*, Doctor?
MARTIN. Yes. Why?
LAVINIA. Oh—nothing.
MARTIN (*to Mary*) The police surgeon's sent it away to be analysed. Then you didn't know there was any whisky in the house?
MARY. No. No—I didn't.
MARTIN. None of you knew?
JANET (*hesitantly*) Yes, I had some sent me this afternoon. (*She rises, moves to the chest of drawers and picks up the bottle of whisky*) A Christmas present. Here it is.
MARTIN. You've been sampling it already, I see. Quite a lot's gone. (*He takes the bottle from Janet*)
JANET. Yes, now you mention it. Oh, dear, it's all very difficult.
MARTIN. Difficult? In what way, Miss Bowering?
RUTH. Miss Bowering means she finds it difficult to tell you that while we were out, Mrs Trellington helped herself.
MARTIN. Really, Mrs Prendergast. Surely that's not true, Mary?
MARY. Yes. I'm afraid it is.
RUTH. She was in the habit of helping herself to anything she fancied.
MARTIN (*moving down* R *and putting the bottle on the table as he passes*) Ladies, I wonder if I could have a word with Mary alone?
RUTH (*rising*) Yes—yes, of course. We can go to my room. Janet, Lavinia. Come along.

(LAVINIA *rises*)

MARTIN. Thank you.

(RUTH, JANET *and* LAVINIA *exit up* L)

(*He crosses down* LC) Mary, darling, I can't tell you how sorry I am about this. Of course, you've nothing to worry about, darling. That is, if . . .
MARY. If what?
MARTIN (*moving to* L *of Mary*) Well, I've a feeling you're holding something back. It may be my imagination, I admit, but the police are bound to ask a lot of questions. Some of them may be a little difficult to answer, and if you tell me everything, it may save a lot of time and trouble.
MARY. But I have told you everything, Martin.
MARTIN. It's really true that Mrs Trellington used to steal from the old ladies?
MARY. Yes.
MARTIN. Mary, darling, I must just ask you this. You knew she was likely to steal Miss Bowering's whisky?

MARY. She always had done, on other occasions.
MARTIN. But, you see, you said there wasn't any whisky in the house.
MARY. There wasn't—not in our part of the house.
MARTIN. But you did know about Miss Bowering's bottle?
MARY. Yes.

(MARTIN *moves to the* R *window*)

MARTIN (*after a pause*) That cat? What happened to the poor thing?
MARY (*rising and moving* L *of Martin*) I buried it in the garden, while they were at the carols. Does it matter?
MARTIN. Yes—yes. I'm afraid it does.

(*There is a knock on the door*)

(*He calls*) Come in.

(DETECTIVE INSPECTOR BRUTON *enters up* L. *He is a very heavily built man of about thirty-five years*)

There you are, Inspector.

(*The* INSPECTOR *closes the door and moves to* L *of Mary*)

Mary, you know Detective Inspector Bruton, don't you?
INSPECTOR (*shaking hands with Mary*) Good evening, Miss Trellington. I'm very sorry to bother you. I quite realize how you must be feeling, but there are one or two things I shall have to ask you. (*He indicates the chair above the table*) Won't you sit down?

(MARY *crosses and sits above the table*)

The doctor has told me as much as he can, and I just want to check up. I understand you went shopping this afternoon?
MARY. Yes.
INSPECTOR (*sitting* L *of the table*) Alone?
MARY. No, I went with my stepmother. But she came home early and I did the rest of the shopping by myself.
INSPECTOR. I see. We found a basket of groceries in the kitchen. I take it they were your purchases?
MARY. Probably. I put it there when I came in. There was nothing we wanted urgently.
INSPECTOR (*producing a piece of paper*) I found this on top of the basket. It's a shopping list. Is this your writing?
MARY. No, my stepmother's. She wrote down everything she wanted me to buy.
INSPECTOR. Including the zinc phosphide? (*To Martin*) I've managed to get Mr Conway on the phone, Doctor, and he confirms the purchase of Miss Trellington. (*To Mary*) It was on the list?

MARY. Yes.
INSPECTOR. Are you sure of that, Miss Trellington?
MARY. Yes. Why do you ask?
INSPECTOR. Because I'm afraid it isn't.

(MARTIN *moves and stands up* R *of Mary*)

MARY. But it must be. (*She snatches the list from the Inspector*) I'm sure it was. (*She looks at the list*) Then I must have been mistaken. (*Suddenly*) Oh, no, I remember now. My stepmother reminded me about it, just as she was leaving me.
INSPECTOR. Oh. (*After a short pause*) Was anyone present when she asked you to get the zinc phosphide—any third party?
MARY. No.
INSPECTOR. I see. And after you bought the stuff and signed the poison book—you said it was for killing rats, didn't you—what did you do with it?
MARY. I put it in the shopping basket with the rest of the things.
INSPECTOR. Was that wise? You work at the hospital, I understand. You must have known it was a dangerous poison.
MARY. I didn't think of it that way. Besides, it was most carefully wrapped, labelled as poison, and the package sealed by Mr Conway himself.
INSPECTOR. Quite. So you brought it back in the basket. What did you do with it then?
MARY. I left it in the basket.
INSPECTOR. Well, it's not there now. Everything on the shopping list is there safely enough, but no zinc phosphide. Haven't you any idea what happened to it?
MARY. No, I'm afraid not, But I did see her open a packet of crystals and turn them into a basin. Then she poured boiling water on them. I was passing through the scullery at the time.
INSPECTOR. And you're sure it was the packet of zinc phosphide she opened?
MARY. Yes, I think it must have been.
INSPECTOR. I wonder what happened to the rest of the packet?
MARY. I don't know. I'm afraid I wasn't taking much notice. But I do remember seeing some of the crystals spilt on the table. Perhaps that's the explanation. Some of the crystals must have fallen by accident into something she ate or drank. It all fits in, doesn't it?
INSPECTOR (*rising*) It's a possibility—yes. However, before we go any farther, Miss Trellington, I think it would be a good idea to have a talk with the other ladies. Excuse me.

(*The* INSPECTOR *crosses and exits up* L)

MARTIN (*moving close to Mary*) Darling, for heaven's sake be careful. Be sure you can verify everything you say. For instance, you said the zinc phosphide was on the shopping list, and it wasn't.

MARY. But I thought it was. It's so difficult to remember tiny details.
MARTIN. But, Mary, you must. You can see the implications—accident, suicide—or murder.

(*The* INSPECTOR *enters up* L *and holds the door open.* MARTIN *moves down* R)

INSPECTOR. Come in, please.

(RUTH, JANET *and* LAVINIA *enter up* L)

Sit down, won't you?

(RUTH *sits in the armchair.* JANET *crosses and sits* R *of the table.* LAVINIA *crosses and sits* L *of the table*)

(*He moves to the fireplace*) Now, as I've just told Miss Trellington, before we go any further, I think it might help if we have a talk, all of us. You all know what's happened—and there are one or two things I'd like to get clear, if you can help me, and I'm sure you will.
RUTH. We'll do what we can.
INSPECTOR. Thank you. First, let's take the possibility of suicide. Can any of you suggest a reason—signs of depression, for example?
RUTH. The doctor has already asked us that. No, none.
INSPECTOR. What do you think, Miss Trellington?
MARY. She seemed perfectly normal.
INSPECTOR. Any money worries?
MARY. On the contrary, she was quite comfortably off.
INSPECTOR. This house belonged to her, I take it?
MARY. Yes. My father left her everything, for life.
INSPECTOR. For life? In trust, I suppose. And on her death?
MARY. It comes to me.
INSPECTOR. You only? No brothers or sisters or other relations to share it?
MARY. None.
INSPECTOR. I understand. Well now, you say Mrs Trellington seemed quite normal today. There were no quarrels or upsets?

(LAVINIA *looks at Janet and the* INSPECTOR *notices*)

(*He crosses to* L *of Lavinia*) You agree, Mrs . . . ?
LAVINIA. *Miss* Goldsworthy.
INSPECTOR. I beg your pardon.
LAVINIA. Well, Mrs Trellington was rather *difficult* at times.
JANET. She had a quick temper.
INSPECTOR (*moving to* L *of Mary*) Was there any trouble today, by any chance?
MARY. It had nothing to do with the ladies, Inspector—at

least not directly. My stepmother and I had a quarrel this afternoon, which they couldn't help overhearing, I'm afraid.

(*There is a knock at the door. The* INSPECTOR *crosses and opens it*)

SERGEANT (*off*) Excuse me, sir.
INSPECTOR. Yes, Sergeant. What is it?
SERGEANT (*off*) Dr Brownlie would like to speak to Miss Trellington downstairs.
INSPECTOR. Very well. (*He turns to* MARY) The police surgeon would like a few words with you, Miss Trellington.

(MARY *rises and moves to the door up* L)

MARTIN (*crossing to the door up* L) I'll come with you.

(MARY, MARTIN *and the* INSPECTOR *exit up* L. *Alone together,* RUTH, LAVINIA *and* JANET *look aghast at each other*)

LAVINIA. Do you think he suspects Mary? That's *impossible*. He couldn't.
RUTH (*rising and moving to* L *of Lavinia*) My dear Lavinia, it's pretty obvious that he does.
LAVINIA. But he couldn't suspect anyone like Mary of killing her stepmother.
RUTH. Try to look at it from his point of view. Mary said that her stepmother had bought the poison. (*She moves and sits above the table*) It was because of that that we—I—made our original plan. She was alone in the house—and she benefits in every way.
LAVINIA. You don't mean that *you* think she did it?
RUTH. What *I* think is beside the point. But the fact that Mary bought the poison, and told the lie about it, is enough to put her under grave suspicion. And suppose—only suppose—she actually *did* what we lacked the courage to do?
LAVINIA. *I'm* wondering if Mary is trying to save *us*.
JANET. You mean—she may think *we* are the ones to blame?
LAVINIA. Why not? Remember, she saw us with that poisoned water and the whisky—just before the carol service. Mary has always tried to protect us, and I think, even if she thought we'd done this dreadful thing, she'd still try to help us.
RUTH. And, in a way, *we* benefit by Mrs Trellington's death.
LAVINIA. Yes and—she knew about Tabitha—how upset we were. And she explained why she said what she did about buying the poison. It was to spare my feelings.
JANET. I believe Miss Goldsworthy's right. Mary is trying to protect us.
RUTH. Yes.
LAVINIA. Then we must tell her at once—explain that we had nothing to do with it.
RUTH. Explaining that would only be throwing more suspicion

on Mary. You see, if it were murder, it can only have been one of the four of us. And Janet! Lavinia! Suppose we are to blame, after all. Those bottles of whisky. Is it possible you made a mistake? Suppose you threw away the wrong bottle—the *unpoisoned* one?

JANET. Oh, no. That's quite absurd. Besides, Miss Goldsworthy was here, too. (*To Lavinia*) Weren't you? You *saw* me do it.

LAVINIA. Yes—yes. I suppose I did. At least, I saw you empty one of the bottles.

RUTH. But which? You were a little excited—even a little hazy perhaps.

LAVINIA. I know. I was feeling most peculiar.

RUTH. Janet. This second bottle—did you take it out of the package before you opened the cupboard—or after?

JANET. After.

LAVINIA. No—before. At least, I think so. Because you showed it to me—and then suggested we changed over. And I held it in my hands.

JANET (*rising*) No—(*she moves to the foot of the bed*) because I fetched it from the bed and held it in *my* hands. (*She moves to R of the table*)

RUTH. Which bottle did you hold in your hands?

JANET } (*together*) { The good one.
LAVINIA }   { The bad one.

RUTH. Well—make up your minds.

LAVINIA. I'm quite certain. I gave the bad bottle to Janet.

JANET. You didn't give it to me. I took it from you.

RUTH. But which one, Janet?

JANET (*moving towards the scullery door*) The one I poured down the sink.

LAVINIA. No, Janet—it was the good bottle—the one you put back in the cupboard that you took from me.

JANET (*moving to R of the table*) But that was after...

RUTH. After what?

LAVINIA (*completely bewildered*) Janet, what was it after?

RUTH. There you are, you see. You're not certain, either of you. And if you did make a mistake over the bottles, it would explain everything.

JANET (*sitting R of the table*) Then what ought we to do?

RUTH. Find out the truth. Mary's in grave danger. There's enough evidence against her for an arrest—even for a conviction.

LAVINIA. You mean Mary might be accused of something we did?

RUTH. Yes.

LAVINIA. Oh, no. We couldn't allow that to happen.

RUTH. Then we must make absolutely certain that Janet didn't make a mistake over the bottles.

JANET. But how? They all look so alike—these whisky bottles. (*She picks up the bottle of whisky from the table, removes the cork and sniffs the bottle*) This doesn't *smell* of anything—except whisky.

(RUTH *takes the bottle from Janet and sniffs it*)

LAVINIA. It's very difficult, isn't it? I really don't see how we *can* tell.

RUTH (*firmly*) I do.

(JANET *and* LAVINIA *look at Ruth*)

The only way to prove if this whisky is poisoned or not is to drink it ourselves.

LAVINIA (*after a pause*) But then—if it *is* poisoned?

RUTH. Isn't it better for us to die than Mary?

LAVINIA (*frightened*) I . . . (*She suddenly realizes the truth*) Yes—yes—I suppose so. Yes—you're right.

RUTH. Janet?

(JANET *does not answer*)

Or are you afraid?

JANET. Afraid? No, no—at least, not very.

RUTH (*quietly*) Good. We're agreed.

JANET (*rising*) I'll get the glasses.

(JANET *exits to the scullery and re-enters immediately with three tumblers*)

Oh dear, I haven't had time to wash them up, I'm afraid. Now I wonder which was mine and which was yours, Mrs Prendergast.

RUTH. In the circumstances, I don't think it really matters.

JANET. No—perhaps not. (*She puts the glasses on the table*)

(RUTH *rises and pours three generous tots of whisky*)

Not too much for me.

RUTH. This is not a social occasion, Janet. (*She hands a glass each to Janet and Lavinia*) Janet! Lavinia!

(LAVINIA *rises. They are about to drink*)

LAVINIA. Perhaps we ought to say good-bye.

RUTH. Good-bye?

LAVINIA. Well, yes—if we're going to . . .

RUTH. Oh, yes yes. I see what you mean. Good-bye, Lavinia. Good-bye, Janet.

JANET (*very frightened*) I never thought . . . But, yes. It's our duty. Good-bye, Mrs Prendergast. Good-bye, Miss Goldsworthy.

LAVINIA. God bless you both.

RUTH. I'll drink first.

JANET. Oh, no—let me. If there was a mistake over the bottles, it was mine.

LAVINIA. I'm equally to blame, I was *with* you.
RUTH. Well, don't let's argue about it. We'll all drink together. Now.

(*They drink.* JANET *and* LAVINIA *cough*)

LAVINIA. It's very strong, isn't it? Much stronger than it was before.
RUTH. Before. Before what?
LAVINIA. Before we sent to the carol service.
RUTH. Oh, yes.
JANET. We had water with it then. (*She moves towards the scullery door*) Perhaps . . .
RUTH (*excited by the drama of the situation*) No—no. Better to finish quickly.

(*They all take another long drink. There is a long pause as they look enquiringly at each other*)

Oh, dear. (*Anxiously*) Are you feeling ill?
LAVINIA. No, no. I don't think so. Not exactly ill. (*She sits* L *of the table*)

(JANET *takes another drink, then sits* R *of the table*)

JANET. Whatever it is, it's working very quickly.

(RUTH *takes another drink, then sits abruptly above the table*)

LAVINIA (*putting a hand over her eyes*) Dear me!
RUTH. It's a strange feeling, isn't it?
LAVINIA. Very. I've never felt anything like it before.
RUTH. I think I have. (*She rises and moves to* R *of Janet*) It takes me back to when I was quite a girl—at a ball. It was soon after I was married. We'd all been to the Viceroy's garden party. There was a young man—and he had a moustache—a very big moustache. He escorted me to the conservatory—but when we arrived—my husband was there. (*She giggles a little and then becomes serious again*) Yes, life was very gay then. (*She moves to the bed and lies on it*)
LAVINIA (*sipping*) I feel now—as though *I'd* had a gay life, too—but I haven't, you know. Many people would have called it a dull one, I suppose. (*She sips*) But, looking back—there was Mr Roberts, my father's curate, you know. *Very* good-looking, he was. But not the marrying kind, I'm afraid. He always seemed more interested in his work and the choir.
RUTH. Poor Lavinia! You never told me about him.

(JANET *takes a drink, laughs and rises*)

JANET. Do you know what I wanted to be when I was a girl? I wanted to be a ballet dancer.

(RUTH *sits up and laughs hysterically*)

RUTH. I've just thought of something—we ought to write a confession—while there's still time.

JANET (*moving to the chest of drawers*) How silly of us to forget. (*She takes a writing pad and fountain pen from the drawer*)

LAVINIA. Yes—must write a confession. Otherwise—I mean, without a confession—the whole thing's—null and void.

RUTH. What? What's null and void?

LAVINIA. I mean, if we don't tell them, they won't understand, will they? We'll be null and void.

JANET (*moving to the bed*) Will you write it, Mrs Prendergast? (*She offers the pad to Ruth*)

RUTH. No. No—I can't.

JANET. Never mind. (*She sits above the table*) I'll write it.

RUTH. We must tell them everything—about Tabitha being poisoned—and the rents.

(JANET *writes.* LAVINIA *dreamily and automatically takes another sip of whisky as she watches Janet*)

LAVINIA. It's quite a long story, isn't it?

(*There is a silence as* RUTH *and* LAVINIA *watch Janet writing the confession. They are sipping pretty steadily and getting sleepier and sleepier*)

RUTH. Say we hoped to put matters right——

JANET (*repeating as she writes*) ". . . we hoped to put matters right . . ."

RUTH. —but inad—by mistake——

JANET. ". . . . but by mistake . . ."

RUTH (*lying back*) —we threw away the wrong bottle.

JANET (*writing*) ". . . we threw away the wrong bottle."

RUTH (*beginning to sag; wearily*) That'll do. We'll have to sign it.

LAVINIA (*sleepily*) Oh, yes. We mustn't forget to sign it—or it'll be null and void. (*She takes the pen and pad from Janet and signs the confession, then returns it to Janet*)

(JANET *signs and offers the pen to Ruth*)

JANET. Mrs Prendergast.

(RUTH *does not reply*)

(*Worried*) Mrs Prendergast.

RUTH (*sitting up*) What?

JANET. Please come and sign.

RUTH. Sign. (*She rises, moves to* R *of the table and signs the confession*)

LAVINIA (*leaning back in her chair*) Oh, dear. I feel so tired—so very tired. (*She closes her eyes and seems to fall asleep*)

JANET (*leaning a little towards Lavinia; anxiously*) Are you in pain?

LAVINIA. No—no pain—I feel very happy. (*Her head goes down on to her arms*)

RUTH (*crossing and standing above Lavinia*) Lavinia! Lavinia—are you dead?

LAVINIA (*very faintly*) Yes. I suppose I am.

RUTH (*moving c; frightened*) Oh, dear! Already. I do think you might have waited. (*She drinks, then flops into the armchair*)

They are all asleep as—

the CURTAIN *falls*

ACT III

SCENE—*The same. Eleven p.m. the same evening.*

When the CURTAIN *rises, the scene is just the same as at the previous Act.* JANET *is asleep on the chair above the table,* LAVINIA *is asleep on the chair* L *of the table and* RUTH *is asleep in the armchair. The* INSPECTOR *is standing up* R *of the table, reading the confession.* DR BROWNLIE, *the police surgeon, is standing at the fireplace, warming his hands.*

INSPECTOR (*moving* C) Well, well, well! (*He glances at the confession again and holds it out to the surgeon*) What do you make of this, Dr Brownlie?

(*The* SURGEON *moves to* L *of the Inspector, takes the confession and reads it. The* INSPECTOR *looks down at the Old Ladies with a chuckle, then takes a small box of mints from his pocket, and swallows one*)

SURGEON (*after a pause*) Well, Bruton—I hardly know. Has it any direct bearing on Mrs Trellington's death, do you think?
INSPECTOR. None at all.
SURGEON. But if they did poison the whisky . . . ?
INSPECTOR. They threw it away. That's quite clear. *And* they didn't make any mistake about the bottles. That's clearer still.
SURGEON (*glancing down at the confession*) H'm. I suppose so.
INSPECTOR. Of course it is, Doctor. If they *had* made a mistake —thrown away the unpoisoned whisky, and drunk the other, they'd be dead by now, wouldn't they? And they're *not* dead.

(JANET *snores*)

At least, they don't sound it to me.
SURGEON. They're not. They're tight—tight as ticks—that's all.
INSPECTOR. Isn't that a bit odd? Only half a bottle of Scotch. D'you really think that just half a bottle . . . ?
SURGEON. Odd by your standards, Bruton. But they don't belong to the Police Club, remember. They're old—and not used to strong drink. And from what Dr Brentwood has told me, probably under-nourished, poor souls.
INSPECTOR. Of course, sir—you know best. (*He takes another mint*)
SURGEON. What's that you keep on taking?
INSPECTOR (*showing the tin to the Surgeon*) Frightful indigestion— or something. (*He gives the slightest of hiccups*) You ought to know. You gave them to me.
SURGEON (*glancing at the tin*) Oh. Well, don't make a habit of it.

RUTH (*slowly but distinctly*) No, Lady Kenwyn.

(*The* INSPECTOR *and the* SURGEON *move up* LC *and look at Ruth*)

I shall *not* be going to His Excellency's garden party this year.
LAVINIA (*moving her head a little*) What did you say?
RUTH. I shall not be going to His Excellency's garden party this year.
LAVINIA. In *that* case—neither shall I.

(RUTH *settles into a more comfortable position and they relapse into unconsciousness again*)

SURGEON (*chuckling*) There you are, Bruton—what did I tell you? Then this doesn't get us any further?
INSPECTOR. Not a yard. Merely the elimination of a possible explanation.
SURGEON. And you still suspect the girl—Miss Trellington?
INSPECTOR (*moving to* R *of the table; cautiously*) Hardly "suspect" —at least, not to the extent of bringing a charge. (*He takes his handkerchief from his pocket and picks up the whisky bottle with it*) But she certainly had a motive. She benefits from her stepmother's death—and they were on bad terms. Also, she works at the hospital and, presumably, knows something about poisons. She bought the stuff this afternoon, and was alone in the house with Mrs Trellington this evening.
SURGEON. Circumstantial—to say the least of it.
INSPECTOR (*moving to the scullery door*) What's more—there's something odd about her general attitude.

(*The* INSPECTOR *exits to the scullery and re-enters almost immediately*)

Dr Brentwood's noticed it, too, although he's pretending he hasn't. (*He crosses to the Surgeon*) These misstatements of hers— saying her stepmother bought the poison—things like that.

(*The* SURGEON *hands the confession to the Inspector*)

(*He puts the confession into his pocket*) If only we could lay our hands on that packet of zinc phosphide—or what's left of it—we might get somewhere.
SURGEON. Your chaps are still searching?
INSPECTOR. Yes—but no luck so far. (*He crosses to the door up* L *and turns*) I suppose they'll be all right? (*He indicates the Old Ladies*)
SURGEON. Quite. I'll get Dr Brentwood to look at them, later on. They're *his* patients. (*He follows the Inspector to the door*)

(*The* INSPECTOR *switches off the lights*)

Better leave the lights on.

(*The* INSPECTOR *switches on the lights*)

If they wake up in the dark and see that fire, it might scare the pants off them.

(*The* INSPECTOR *and the* SURGEON *exit up* L)

RUTH (*waking up*) Who's flicking those lights? (*She pauses*) Lavinia! Janet! Janet!

JANET (*waking with a start*) Yes. What is it?

RUTH. Wake up, Lavinia.

LAVINIA (*waking slowly*) Did someone speak?

RUTH. *I* did.

LAVINIA. Oh, yes. Something about a garden party. (*She puts her hands to her head*) Oh, dear!

JANET (*vaguely*) Good morning.

RUTH. What?

JANET. I said "good morning".

LAVINIA. Is it morning? Oh, yes—I suppose it must be.

RUTH. Does it matter?

LAVINIA. Oh, yes. Only I can't remember why.

JANET. I can. If it's morning, it's Christmas Day—and we must wish each other a Merry Christmas.

RUTH. Merry? I don't feel in the least bit merry.

LAVINIA. Neither do I. Oh, my poor head.

RUTH. That's the whisky we drank.

LAVINIA. Whisky? I never drink whisky. Oh, yes—why did we?

RUTH (*rising and moving to* L *of Lavinia*) Lavinia! Janet! Don't you realize what's happened? We're alive. (*She puts her hand to her head*)

LAVINIA. Are we? Oh, yes—so we are.

JANET. Is that good or bad?

RUTH (*moving to* L *of Janet*) Oh, do try and pull yourselves together. Don't you understand what it means?

JANET. No—not quite.

RUTH. It means that the whisky we drank wasn't poisoned. Janet didn't make a mistake over the bottles.

JANET. Oh, dear. I almost wish I had.

RUTH (*crossing above Janet to* R *of her*) Don't be absurd, Janet. The whisky in that cupboard wasn't poisoned, and so we had nothing to do with Mrs Trellington's death.

JANET. Then—doesn't that prove . . . ? I mean—if she *was* murdered—that Mary must have had something to do with it?

LAVINIA. Oh—no.

RUTH (*very gravely*) It doesn't prove it—but I see what you mean.

JANET (*suddenly alert*) Where's the confession we wrote? We must destroy it. It was here on the table.

RUTH. Well, it's not here now. (*She begins searching around*) Have *you* had it, Lavinia?

(JANET *rises*)

LAVINIA (*rising*) No.
RUTH. We *must* find it—it can't be far away. (*She looks on the bedside table*)
LAVINIA. Perhaps someone's taken it.
RUTH. How could they? We were here alone.
JANET. Perhaps someone could have come in while we were asleep.
LAVINIA. Oh, dear. hope not. (*She moves to the armchair*) To be seen—as we were.
RUTH. It's probably dropped on the floor.
LAVINIA. On the floor!

(*All three of them start searching under the table and chairs.* RUTH *kneels by the bed.* JANET *kneels below the table and* LAVINIA *kneels and looks under the armchair.*
MARTIN *enters up* L *and moves* C)

MARTIN (*astonished*) What on earth are you doing?
RUTH. We're looking for something, Doctor—something we've mislaid.
MARTIN. I see. Well, the police surgeon sent me up. He thought I'd better have a look at you. (*He moves to Ruth*) Oh, by the way, Mrs Prendergast, if it's your letter you're looking for, it's quite all right. The Inspector's got it.
RUTH. He hasn't *read* it?
MARTIN. Yes. So have I. (*He assists Ruth to rise*) Take my advice and come downstairs.

(JANET *and* LAVINIA *rise.* LAVINIA *sits on the right arm of the armchair*)

A cup of tea will make you all feel better.

(MARY *enters up* L)

(*He moves to* R *of Mary*) Ah, Mary. Is there any tea going downstairs?
MARY. Yes, of course.
MARTIN. I think it would do us all good.
LAVINIA. Tea? (*She rises and moves towards the door up* L. *Over her shoulder*) I should love a cup of tea.

(*The* INSPECTOR *enters up* L. LAVINIA *bumps into him*)

(*She reacts nervously*) Oh, tea!

(LAVINIA *exits up* L. RUTH *crosses above the others to* L *of the Inspector*)

INSPECTOR. So you're feeling better, eh, Mrs Prendergast?
RUTH. That, Inspector, is entirely a matter of opinion.

(RUTH *exits up* L)

JANET (*hurrying after Ruth*) Mrs Prendergast! Miss Goldsworthy! Don't leave me here alone.

(JANET *exits up* L. MARY *is about to follow, but the* INSPECTOR *closes the door*)

INSPECTOR. I'm sorry to be a nuisance, Miss Trellington, but I'd like to go back to this business of the zinc phosphide. (*He moves to the fireplace*) You say you saw your stepmother open it and empty the crystals into a basin?
MARY. Yes.
INSPECTOR. And it was the same packet you bought at Conway's this afternoon?
MARY (*moving above the armchair*) Naturally.
MARTIN (*moving to* R *of Mary*) Why are you asking this, Inspector?
INSPECTOR. Because, Dr Brentwood, Sergeant Rawlings has just given me this packet, found at the top of the cellar stairs. (*He produces a small white packet from his pocket*) This is a packet of zinc phosphide—and there can be no doubt it's the one Miss Trellington bought this afternoon. (*He reads*) "Zinc Phosphide. Poison." The prescription number's here and today's date.
MARY. There you are, you see. That's what happened to the rest of it.
INSPECTOR. Not the rest of it, Miss Trellington—*all* of it. (*Gravely*) This packet hadn't been opened. The seals are intact. (*He holds out the packet to Mary*) You can see. (*He crosses and stands down* R)

(MARY *looks from Martin to the Inspector*)

A very ingenious theory, Miss Trellington, but I'm afraid it's not the answer. We found a bowl of ordinary fruit jelly in the kitchen. That's what you saw your stepmother making. But it hasn't been touched. The poison which killed Mrs Trellington was not the zinc phosphide you bought this afternoon.
MARY (*moving to the fireplace*) In that case, Inspector, I can't help you any more.
INSPECTOR. *Can't* you, Miss Trellington? Then I'm afraid I shall have to ask you to come along to the police station.
MARY. The police . . . ?
MARTIN (*moving to* L *of the table*) Why—that's absurd, Inspector.
INSPECTOR. I don't see it that way. You're a professional man yourself. You must realize that I have a duty to do. (*He crosses below Martin to* L *of him*) I can't allow myself to be influenced by personal considerations.
MARTIN. And as a professional man, I would like to suggest that it's a very unwise thing to subject Miss Trellington to a

further ordeal, after what she's been through. Surely you can wait till you have an analysis of the whisky found by Mrs Trellington's bedside? Isn't that the key to the whole problem?

INSPECTOR. In a way, perhaps.

MARTIN. Couldn't you ring through, from the box outside, and find out if the report is in yet?

INSPECTOR. Very well, Doctor. I'm sure I don't want to make things more difficult for this lady than is absolutely necessary. (*He moves to the door up* L) In the meantime, I must ask you not to leave the house. Can I have your guarantee of that, Doctor?

MARTIN. Certainly.

MARY. I'm not going to run away.

INSPECTOR. Of course not, Miss Trellington. In the circumstances, that would be a very unwise thing to do, wouldn't it?

(*The* INSPECTOR *exits up* L. *The church clock off strikes the half hour*)

MARY (*crossing to the* R *window*) It's getting terribly late.

MARTIN (*moving to the fireplace*) Yes. Half past eleven. Nearly Christmas Day.

MARY (*glancing out of the window*) People are just arriving at St Jude's for the midnight service.

MARTIN. Yes—I suppose they are.

MARY (*after a pause*) I think it's going to snow. (*She moves* C) We were going to church this evening, weren't we?

MARTIN. Yes. I was looking forward to it. Mary, darling—before the Inspector comes back, can't you tell me? I know you're hiding something.

MARY (*sitting on the right arm of the armchair*) I've told you all I can, Martin.

MARTIN (*sitting on the left arm of the armchair*) But some of the things you've said weren't true, and I want to know why you said them.

MARY. They *were* true, Martin. Except right at the beginning, when I said my stepmother had bought the zinc phosphide herself.

MARTIN. But this business of the jelly and the crystals?

MARY. I *did* see her dissolving some crystals, and some of them *were* spilt.

MARTIN. But it wasn't the answer, and you know it.

MARY (*rising*) It would have been so much simpler if it had been.

MARTIN (*rising and moving to* L *of Mary*) Then there *is* something else?

MARY (*after a pause*) Oh, Martin—I'm frightened—so terribly frightened.

MARTIN. What is it, Mary?

MARY. I know I can trust you—but if I tell you something, you

won't have to pass it on to the police, will you—your duty as a doctor—or anything like that?
MARTIN. Of course not, darling. You can tell me anything. But I must know the truth.
MARY. It's the old ladies.
MARTIN. What about them?
MARY. I believe they did it. They *must* have done—out of sheer desperation. You see, I actually saw them doing something to the whisky, just before they went out this evening.
MARTIN. But, Mary, darling . . .
MARY. They were quite certain my stepmother would steal it—and they were right. She did. They were desperate at the thought of being turned out. They weren't *responsible*, were they?
MARTIN. And this is why you've been inventing stories to Bruton? You've been trying to put him off the scent?
MARY. Yes. I've been trying to help them. Don't you see?
MARTIN. Yes—yes, darling. I do. (*He crosses and stands below the table*) But, oh, Mary!
MARY. What?
MARTIN. In trying to help them, you've . . . (*He leans on the table*) Darling, before the old ladies drank the rest of the whisky and passed out, they left a note—wrote a confession.
MARY. A confession?
MARTIN. They meant it as a confession, and it seems to have convinced the Inspector that they had nothing to do with Mrs Trellington's death at all.
MARY. But then—who?
MARTIN. Yes—who? (*He rises and moves down* R) There were only four of you in the house, just before it happened.
MARY (*crossing to* L *of Martin*) Martin—you don't think *I* murdered her? Is that what you're trying to say? That I did it?
MARTIN. No, of course not. But—this confession. I wonder if the old ladies have written it as a bluff—that they've been fooling us?

(JANET *and* LAVINIA *enter up* L)

JANET (*crossing to* C) Excuse me. May we come in?

(LAVINIA *stands* L *of Janet.*
RUTH *enters up* L *and moves to the fireplace*)

MARTIN. Yes, of course. How are you all feeling?
RUTH. Better, thank you, decidedly better.
LAVINIA. It was an extraordinary experience—most extraordinary.
JANET. But if the whisky hadn't been so strong, it would have been quite enjoyable. I wonder what's happened to the rest of that bottle we were drinking?
MARTIN. The whisky? The Inspector's taken it.

JANET. Taken it? Do you mean he's *drunk* it?
MARTIN. No. He's just taken it away.
JANET. Well! All I can say is, I consider it a liberty.
LAVINIA. So do I.
JANET. He didn't even ask.
LAVINIA. No.
MARTIN. I suppose he considered it was a matter of duty, Miss Bowering, and . . .
JANET (*annoyed*) I really can't see that it was anyone's duty to go off with my whisky, especially as I'd hoped to share the little that was left with my friends on Christmas Day.
LAVINIA (*sitting in the armchair*) That's very kind of you, Janet, but—somehow—I don't think it agrees with me very well.
MARTIN. The Inspector may bring it back. If not, he'll give you a receipt for it.
JANET (*still annoyed*) What's the good of that? A receipt won't warm us up on a cold day.

(*There is a knock on the door*)

(*She calls*) Come in.

(*The* INSPECTOR *enters up* L)

INSPECTOR. Filthy night!
LAVINIA. You mean, it's snowing?

(RUTH *sits on the chair down* L)

INSPECTOR (*moving to the fireplace*) It's going to. (*He warms his hands*) My kids'll be pleased if they wake up and find it's a white Christmas.
JANET. If you've brought my whisky back, I might offer you a little.
INSPECTOR (*crossing to* L *of Janet*) Thank you, ma'am, but I never drink on duty. And the whisky's at the station, I'm afraid.
JANET (*sitting above the table*) Well—really!
INSPECTOR. I'm sorry, madam, but we need the bottles to check up on fingerprints—the fingerprints of all concerned.
LAVINIA. *Our* fingerprints?
INSPECTOR. If you'll be so good as to allow them to be taken.
RUTH. We're not criminals, Inspector. You can't take our fingerprints if we don't want you to.
INSPECTOR. I'm well aware of that, madam. But I'm sure you want to help as much as possible. They're not kept on record, you know. They're destroyed immediately investigations are completed.
RUTH. And if we refuse?
INSPECTOR. It would complicate things a little—cause a slight delay. I should have to get a warrant from a Magistrate's Court. (*He crosses to* L *of Mary*) Miss Trellington, I'm sorry to have to say

this—very sorry indeed—but in view of further evidence, I'm afraid I must ask you to come along to the police station now.

(JANET *rises, moves to the armchair and sits on the right arm*)

MARTIN. But, Inspector—you said you'd wait until you had a report on the analysis of the whisky in the glass.

INSPECTOR. No, Doctor. I said I'd *consider* waiting. The situation has changed a little since then.

MARTIN. You've had the report?

INSPECTOR. Not yet. But I need Miss Trellington for some further enquiries. (*To Mary*) You understand?

MARY. Yes. Shall I—may I—fetch my coat? (*She crosses to the door up* L)

INSPECTOR. Yes—of course.

MARTIN (*crossing to the door up* L) I'll come with you, darling.

INSPECTOR. That's all right, Doctor. My Sergeant will look after her.

(MARY *exits up* L)

MARTIN (*moving to* L *of the Inspector*) This *is* really necessary, of course, Inspector?

INSPECTOR. Yes. (*He moves down* R) I'm not in the habit of doing anything without a good reason.

RUTH. Even to taking our fingerprints?

INSPECTOR. Yes, madam. They'll certainly provide us with indisputable evidence as to who handled those two half bottles of whisky and who didn't. For instance, if it should be proved that Mrs Trellington handled the bottle of good whisky, but did not touch the empty one—the one which had apparently been poisoned—it will help quite a lot.

MARTIN (*moving* C) Well, ladies, it will certainly confirm *your* story, won't it?

RUTH. Most certainly. Did you require such confirmation, Dr Brentwood?

MARTIN. It wouldn't do any harm, would it? (*He moves to* L *of the Inspector*) And if Miss Trellington's fingerprints don't appear on either bottle, it will prove she isn't implicated at all, won't it?

INSPECTOR. Not necessarily, I'm afraid. Already it seems pretty clear that the whisky her stepmother took from Miss Bowering's bottle was perfectly harmless. There is, however, the question of the glass.

MARTIN. What glass?

INSPECTOR. The glass found by Mrs Trellington's bedside. There are several sets of fingerprints on the glass. Two we are certain are female—and one set are definitely those of the deceased lady.

MARTIN. Are you suggesting that the others are those of Miss Trellington?

INSPECTOR. I'm not suggesting anything of the kind, Doctor. But it's another of the things I must find out.

MARTIN. Well, suppose they are. She might have picked up the glass when she found her stepmother dead. Quite a natural thing to do.

INSPECTOR. Possible. But I'm afraid Miss Trellington's evidence has been very unsatisfactory all through. Very little she says can be confirmed.

MARTIN. But suppose the contents of the glass are found to be harmless?

(*There is a knock on the door*)

What then?

(*The* INSPECTOR *crosses to the door up* L *and opens it*)

INSPECTOR. What is it?

SERGEANT (*off*) Excuse me, sir. Will you come and have a look at this?

(*The* INSPECTOR *exits up* L)

LAVINIA. Poor, dear Mary. I'm absolutely certain there's been a dreadful mistake.

JANET. Can't we do *anything*? I'm convinced she had nothing to do with it.

MARTIN. So am I. If only we could find some way of proving it.

(*The* INSPECTOR *enters up* L. *He carries a small trinket box*)

INSPECTOR (*moving* C *and displaying the box*) Have any of you seen this before? (*He sits* L *of the table*)

RUTH. No. No, I don't think so.

MARTIN (*sitting* R *of the table*) What is it, Inspector?

INSPECTOR. A kind of trinket box. It's just been found, hidden away on the top of a wardrobe in Mrs Trellington's room. (*He opens the box and empties out a lot of cheap trinkets on to the table*) Nothing much here. Just a lot of junk. (*He picks up a powder box and examines it*) Powder box. I don't know about this.

MARTIN. Antique, by the look of it.

INSPECTOR. Possibly. I'm afraid I'm no expert.

JANET (*rising and moving above the table; nervously*) Do you mind if I . . . ? (*She indicates the box*) When I was with Lady Glassbury—she was a great collector of such things. (*She holds out her hand*) May I?

INSPECTOR. Certainly. (*He hands Janet the powder box*)

JANET (*examining the powder box*) Oh, yes. It's antique, all right.

(LAVINIA *rises, moves to* L *of the Inspector and looks at the box*)

And Italian, too, unless I'm very much mistaken. (*She opens the*

box) Oh, dear! It's empty. What a pity. (*She is just going to return it to the Inspector when her attention is attracted by a small rattle*) No, I don't think it is. (*She holds the box to her ear and shakes it*) Wait a minute—I remember now. Lady Glassbury bought one of these which . . . (*She fiddles with the box, presses a spring and releases a secret compartment*) Ah, yes. Look. A ring. That's what I heard rattling. (*She holds the ring out to the Inspector*)
INSPECTOR (*taking the ring*) A secret compartment, eh?
JANET. Just like the one Lady Glassbury bought.
LAVINIA (*peering over the Inspector's shoulder*) How clever of you, Janet.

(*The* INSPECTOR *turns his head to Lavinia.* LAVINIA, *startled, backs to the armchair and sits*)

JANET (*very pleased with herself, but determined to be modest*) Well—not exactly *clever*—I just remembered.
MARTIN. Quite a *good* ring, isn't it?
JANET (*before the Inspector can reply*) Oh, yes, Doctor. A very good ring.
INSPECTOR. Very nice indeed. In fact, quite valuable.
RUTH. Remarkable! I never knew the woman possessed any good jewellery.
INSPECTOR. Sapphire—very good colour—surrounded by diamonds—nine of 'em—set in platinum. (*He rises suddenly, crosses to the door up* L *and opens it*)
MARTIN. What is it, Inspector?
INSPECTOR (*calling*) Rawlings!
SERGEANT (*off*) Sir?
INSPECTOR. You know Fawcett's shop? Go round and bring him back here.
SERGEANT (*off*) Right, sir.
INSPECTOR. And tell him it's urgent—that I want him right away.

(*The Old Ladies exchange puzzled glances. The* INSPECTOR *closes the door*)

MARTIN. Why on earth send for Fawcett?
INSPECTOR (*crossing to* L *of the table*) Because of this ring. It looks very much like the one we've been trying to find for the last two months.
RUTH. You mean the one stolen from Mr Fawcett's safe?
INSPECTOR. That's it. (*To Martin*) He may be able to identify it. (*He turns to Ruth*) How did you know about it, madam?
RUTH. Because Mr Fawcett told us himself—how worried he was.
JANET. And how the insurance people and the police are still investigating.
INSPECTOR. I must say, it did look a bit suspicious.

RUTH (*rising and crossing to* L *of the Inspector*) So the police *can* make mistakes, Inspector.

INSPECTOR (*easily*) Oh, yes, madam—sometimes. But not often very serious ones. (*He replaces the ring and slips the box into his pocket*) By the way, when did Mr Fawcett tell you all this?

JANET. This evening, of course.

INSPECTOR. This evening? After Dr Brentwood sent him to phone the police station.

LAVINIA. Oh, no. Before that. When he brought the Christmas cards—and a present for Mrs Trellington.

INSPECTOR. *Before* Mrs Trellington's death?

RUTH. Naturally. It was about five o'clock. (*She sits on the right arm of the armchair*)

INSPECTOR. You didn't tell me—that Mr Fawcett was here then.

RUTH. I don't remember your *asking*, Inspector. It didn't seem to be of any consequence.

INSPECTOR. No? Possibly not.

(MARY *enters up* L. *She wears her coat, and looks very pale and distressed.* MARTIN *rises*)

Ah, here you are, Miss Trellington. We shan't keep you waiting long. (*He takes the box from his pocket and shows it to Mary*) In the meantime, have you ever seen this before?

MARY (*moving to* L *of the Inspector*) Never.

INSPECTOR. Or any of these? (*He shows Mary the trinket box and the oddments of jewellery on the table*)

MARY. Yes. That's my stepmother's trinket box. She's had it for years, though I haven't seen it lately.

INSPECTOR. Tell me—had she any valuable jewellery?

MARY. I don't think so. Only things like that. Nothing worth more than a pound or two.

INSPECTOR. I see. Well, I'm just waiting to have a word with Mr Fawcett. One of my men has gone to fetch him. He shouldn't keep us waiting long.

MARY. Mr Fawcett? (*She crosses to* L *of Martin*) Why, Martin—what's happened?

MARTIN. Never mind about that now, darling. Come and sit down.

(MARY *sits* R *of the table*)

RUTH (*rising and moving to* L *of the Inspector*) Inspector, I think it's disgraceful to take Miss Trellington away like this. Dr Brentwood, surely you're not going to allow it?

INSPECTOR. I'm afraid this matter has passed out of Dr Brentwood's hands. (*He moves below the table*) Miss Trellington, while we're waiting, there's one more question I'd like to ask you.

(RUTH *sits on the right arm of the armchair*)

MARY. Yes?

(JANET *crosses and sits on the left arm of the armchair*)

INSPECTOR. When you went into your stepmother's room this evening, can you tell me exactly what you did? Try and think back. You opened the door and went into the room. Did you expect to find her there?

MARY. No. I thought she was out. I was just going to light the gas fire, when I saw her lying on the bed. At first, I thought she was asleep—then I saw there was something strange about her. She had a magazine in her hand. I took it and . . .

MARTIN (*prompting*) Put it on the bedside table, with the glass.

INSPECTOR (*raising a hand to silence Martin*) Doctor, please. (*To Mary*) Yes, Miss Trellington?

MARY. That's all.

INSPECTOR. What did you do then?

MARY. I rushed up here. (*To the Old Ladies*) That's right, isn't it?

RUTH. Yes, Mary. Of course it is.

INSPECTOR. Did you touch anything else in the room?

MARY. No. At least, I don't think I did.

INSPECTOR. Think very carefully. This is important.

(MARY *tries to concentrate and gazes round at the others, panic-stricken, as they all watch her*)

MARY. It's no good. I can't remember. It was all so horrible.

(*There is a knock on the door*)

INSPECTOR (*calling*) Come in.

(FAWCETT *enters up* L. *He looks very flustered and bears all the signs of having come away in a hurry. His shoes are unlaced and he wears a pyjama jacket tucked into his trousers, which can be seen when he unbuttons his coat. He also wears a scarf*)

FAWCETT (*moving* C) You know, it's really very disturbing being dragged out of bed on a night like this.

INSPECTOR (*moving to* R *of Fawcett*) I'm very sorry.

FAWCETT (*ruffled*) I dare say, Inspector—but to be seen by people coming along the Causeway—at this hour—not properly attired—and with a police officer, too. And I've done everything I possibly can to help you in . . .

INSPECTOR (*calming him down*) Yes, yes, yes. That's just the point. I think we may be in a position to help *you*.

FAWCETT. Help *me*? In what way?

(*The* INSPECTOR *takes the powder box from his pocket, removes the ring and hands it to Fawcett*)

INSPECTOR. Take a look at this.

(FAWCETT *examines the ring*)

Recognize it?

(FAWCETT *fumbles for his spectacles and puts them on*)

FAWCETT. Just a minute, Inspector. Why, good heavens above! This ring is Mrs Fenner-Findlay's.

INSPECTOR. Are you sure of that?

FAWCETT (*examining the ring*) Quite sure. Sapphire and nine diamonds. Not the slightest doubt. I'm *positive*.

INSPECTOR. I thought it might be.

FAWCETT. Where on earth did you find it?

INSPECTOR. Amongst some things of Mrs Trellington's—hidden in this little powder box, in a secret compartment. (*He hands the box to Fawcett*)

FAWCETT. Why, bless my soul! That's the box I gave her last October, after she helped me in the shop—when I was ill.

INSPECTOR. Wasn't that about the time the ring disappeared?

FAWCETT. Come to think of it—yes. But—Mrs *Trellington!* You can't mean . . . ?

INSPECTOR. It seems that Mrs Trellington wasn't above helping herself to anything she fancied.

FAWCETT (*very shocked; incredulously*) Oh, no. Surely not?

RUTH. She was a thief, Mr Fawcett. There's ample proof of that.

FAWCETT. Mrs Trellington—the last person I should have thought of. (*He crosses and sits* L *of the table. Sadly*) And I was getting so fond of her.

INSPECTOR (*taking the ring from Fawcett*) I'd better take charge of the ring for the time being, Mr Fawcett. (*He crosses and stands below the table*) Well now, Miss Trellington, if you're ready, shall we go along?

(MARY *rises*)

FAWCETT. Surely you're not going out again, at this time of night?

RUTH. The Inspector insists on taking Miss Trellington along to the police station. First he suspects you of stealing that ring— now he suspects Mary of murdering her stepmother.

INSPECTOR. Steady, Mrs Prendergast. You're saying that, not me. (*He helps himself to another tablet from his tin*)

FAWCETT. The box, Inspector. You'll want to take it with you, I expect. Just a minute. There seems to be something else here.

INSPECTOR (*taking the powder box from Fawcett*) Let's see. Yes, caught up at the back. A screw of paper. (*He opens the paper*) One of your billheads, by the look of it.

FAWCETT (*rising*) What?

INSPECTOR. One of your billheads, Mr Fawcett. And some crystals of some sort.
FAWCETT. Crystals?
INSPECTOR. Yes. (*He holds out the screw of paper*)
FAWCETT (*excitedly*) Inspector, those crystals are cyanide. (*He moves to* L *of the Inspector and looks closely at the crystals*) Cyanide of potassium.
MARTIN (*stepping forward*) Cyanide?
FAWCETT. Yes, Doctor. Potassium cyanide. I use it sometimes —for my work.
INSPECTOR. I see. Where do you buy it?
FAWCETT. Conway's—of course.
INSPECTOR. When did you last use any of it?
FAWCETT. It must have been about two months ago. But the funny thing is that I wanted some only the other day, and found I had none left. I was surprised, because I felt pretty certain I still had some.

(*The* INSPECTOR *takes an envelope from his wallet and puts the crystals into it*)

INSPECTOR. So the cyanide disappeared—just as the ring disappeared?
FAWCETT. Yes.
INSPECTOR. And presumably about the same time?
FAWCETT. It *could* have been.
INSPECTOR. Then—when Mrs Trellington stole the ring, she could have taken the cyanide as well?
FAWCETT. It looks as if she must have done. But *why*? What could she possibly want with deadly stuff like that?
RUTH. I think I can answer that, Mr Fawcett. She probably took it to kill your dog.
FAWCETT. To kill Chummy? Oh, no, Mrs Prendergast. I really can't believe that. She always seemed so fond of animals.
RUTH. You're wrong, Mr Fawcett. She *hated* animals. This evening, after you'd gone, we found that she'd poisoned Tabitha.
FAWCETT (*flabbergasted*) No. (*He looks towards Lavinia for confirmation*) Oh, my dear Miss Goldsworthy, what an awful thing to happen.
LAVINIA. Yes, it was dreadful. Such a shock.
RUTH. Wasn't that how Chummy died—quite suddenly, Mr Fawcett?
FAWCETT. Yes, it was.
RUTH. There you are, then. At first we thought she must have killed Tabitha with the zinc phosphide she asked Mary to buy, but now, since the packet hasn't been opened, and she had this cyanide, it seems to be the answer, doesn't it?

(FAWCETT *crosses and sits on the chair down* L)

FAWCETT. What a wicked, wicked thing!

INSPECTOR. Well, Miss Trellington?

RUTH (*rising and moving* C) But surely, Inspector, you're not taking Miss Trellington to the police station after what we've just found out?

INSPECTOR. I'm sorry, madam, but I must. In view of Miss Trellington's unsatisfactory evidence, it's my duty to do so.

RUTH. But our evidence has been just as unsatisfactory.

LAVINIA. It may be stupid of me, but if Mary goes to the police station, I think we should *all* go.

JANET. Oh, no!

RUTH. Lavinia's right. Besides, it would be very much *nicer* for Mary.

JANET. I'm not going out tonight. Dr Brentwood said I was to be careful of the night air. Didn't you, Doctor?

MARTIN. Well, yes.

INSPECTOR. Nobody's *asking* you to go out, Miss Bowering.

LAVINIA. You know, Janet—I've never been in a Black Mary.

INSPECTOR (*fumbling for his tin of tablets as he gets more and more exasperated*) Miss Goldsworthy, you're not *going* in a Black Maria —none of you. I'm asking *Miss Trellington* to accompany me to the police station.

RUTH. But to accuse her of murder . . .

INSPECTOR. Mrs Prendergast—please don't put words in my mouth. Nobody is accusing Miss Trellington. (*He slips a tablet into his mouth*) It's merely that, in the interest of everyone, I'm obliged to ask Miss Trellington to come to the police station, and, if she wishes, to make a statement.

MARY (*moving to* R *of the Inspector; slightly hysterically*) It's no good. I can't tell you any more than I have. I've told you *everything.* (*She turns and moves to Martin*)

(MARTIN *takes Mary in his arms*)

INSPECTOR. I'm very sorry, Miss Trellington.

RUTH. If Mary goes, *we* go, too—and that's my last word, Inspector. Lavinia! Janet! Come along. (*She moves to the door up* L)

(JANET *and* LAVINIA *rise and move to the door up* L)

INSPECTOR. Mrs Prendergast, will you please come back and sit down. Now listen to me. Hic! (*He hiccups*) I beg your pardon. Hic! Officially I can't stop you going. Hic!

(RUTH *turns and crosses to* L *of the Inspector.* JANET *moves to* L *of Ruth.* LAVINIA *sits on the left arm of the armchair*)

RUTH. Hiccups, Inspector? How very distressing.

INSPECTOR. I'm sorry, Mrs Prendergast—but if I get nervous or irritated . . . Hic!

RUTH. Can't *you* do something, Dr Brentwood?
MARTIN. Well, there are lots of remedies—none of them infallible, I'm afraid.
LAVINIA. Perhaps it would be better if we all went to bed, and you came and saw us in the morning.
INSPECTOR. I have no intention . . . Hic!
JANET. Inspector, you haven't been drinking my whisky, have you?
INSPECTOR. Miss Bowering, I do assure you . . . Hic!
LAVINIA (*rising*) How about a cold key down his back?
RUTH. Lavinia—that's for a bleeding nose.
JANET. Perhaps, if he held his breath?
RUTH. For a very long time.
LAVINIA. I know. A glass of water.
RUTH. Drunk slowly, from the wrong side of the glass. Janet—glass.

(JANET *moves to the cupboard* L, *takes out a glass and gives it to Ruth.* RUTH *hands the glass to* MARTIN, *who gets the jug of water from the bedside table and pours some water into the glass*)

MARTIN. That's as good as anything. (*He hands the glass of water to the Inspector*)
RUTH (*sitting above the table*) Now, Inspector. Bend over and sip. From the wrong side of the glass. Hold your nose.
LAVINIA (*suddenly*) Stop! That water's poisoned.
INSPECTOR. Poisoned?
LAVINIA. Yes. That water—it's poisoned.
JANET. Why, of course. The water in that jug came from Tabitha's drinking bowl. We found it too difficult . . .
LAVINIA. And I said—better pour it into the jug first.
RUTH. And I put that jug on the table—and we forgot all about it—and that's what's left over.
MARTIN. We'd better get this quite clear, Miss Goldsworthy. The water in that jug is the same water that Tabitha drank before you found her dead?
LAVINIA. Yes—yes.
MARTIN. The water that Mrs Trellington poisoned?
LAVINIA. Yes.

(*The* SURGEON *enters up* L)

SURGEON (*crossing to* L *of the Inspector*) Oh, Inspector!
INSPECTOR. What is it, Doctor?
SURGEON. They've completed the analysis of the whisky we found in Mrs Trellington's glass.
INSPECTOR. It contained poison?
SURGEON. It contained poison all right—enough to kill a dozen.
INSPECTOR. Zinc phosphide?

SURGEON. No—potassium cyanide.

(RUTH *rises*)

MARTIN. Cyanide?

INSPECTOR (*handing the jug of water to the Surgeon*) Doctor, would you have this analysed?

SURGEON. Keeping us busy, aren't you?

(*The* SURGEON *exits up* L)

MARTIN. This alters things a bit, doesn't it, Inspector?

INSPECTOR. Does it? Well, I don't quite know.

MARTIN. But it's clearly established that Mrs Trellington was in possession of potassium cyanide at the time of her death, isn't it?

INSPECTOR. But it doesn't mean she took it herself. Someone else may have had access to it. Miss Trellington...

MARY. *I've* never seen the stuff before. I hadn't the slightest idea she had it—I've never even seen the box she kept it in.

INSPECTOR. And you've never bought cyanide yourself, Miss Trellington?

MARY. Never.

INSPECTOR. You're quite *sure?*

MARTIN. If she had, Conway's would have a record of it.

INSPECTOR. Conway's is not the only chemist, and she works at the hospital.

MARY. I've never bought cyanide of potassium anywhere—never. (*She sits* R *of the table*)

MARTIN. Look here, Inspector. The water in that jug was poured from the cat's drinking bowl. Therefore, if Mrs Trellington used cyanide to poison Tabitha, in the same way as she used it to poison Mr Fawcett's dog, that jug contained cyanide, didn't it? You agree?

INSPECTOR. On that point, yes.

(MARTIN *crosses and stands up* LC)

LAVINIA. But if Mrs Trellington used cyanide to poison my little Tabitha, why did she send Mary to buy the... whatever it is?

RUTH. Zinc phosphide, Lavinia. (*She rises and moves to* R *of the Inspector*) I suggest Mrs Trellington wanted that zinc phosphide for the very reason she gave—to kill rats. She already *had* the cyanide to kill poor Tabitha.

INSPECTOR. Maybe. But it doesn't explain how the cyanide got into the whisky she drank.

LAVINIA. Unless she committed suicide. Remorse perhaps—she was sorry she'd killed my poor little cat.

RUTH. *That* I consider most unlikely.

LAVINIA (*twittering on*) But people *do* become sorry all of a sudden, don't they? They set out to do something wicked and then they repent and try to make amends. (*To Janet*) We know that's true, don't we, Janet? My dear father used to say . . .

RUTH (*interrupting*) Please don't chatter, Lavinia.

LAVINIA (*a little piqued*) I'm sorry. I was only trying to help.

RUTH. Then try some other time. Something has just struck me—something that may be very important indeed. Janet—has that jug of poisoned water been standing on the bedside table since before we went to the carol service?

JANET. Yes. It was terribly careless of me, I admit.

LAVINIA. But you forgot all about it, didn't you? And . . .

RUTH. Never mind about that. The point is that the jug was standing there when Mrs Trellington stole your whisky, Janet?

JANET. Why, yes. Certainly.

RUTH. Well, Inspector—surely you see what happened?

INSPECTOR. I'm afraid I don't.

RUTH. I should have thought it was obvious. The unpoisoned whisky was hidden in this cupboard, wasn't it? Very well. Mrs Trellington came into this room and helped herself. Then, presumably, she put the whisky back in the cupboard. You follow? Now, imagine I am Mrs Trellington, standing here with a glass of whisky in my hand. What would I do before drinking it?

LAVINIA. Add water, I hope.

RUTH. Precisely. And there was that jug of water—standing there all ready to hand.

MARTIN (*excitedly*) I see what you're getting at. You mean, Mrs Trellington added water to her whisky from that jug.

RUTH (*nodding*) Water poisoned with cyanide.

MARTIN. But she wasn't to know that. Don't you see, Bruton? She thought it was pure water—made the mistake we all nearly made, a moment ago?

RUTH. She added water from that jug to the whisky she'd stolen—and then took it down to her room to drink at her leisure.

JANET. You mean—she poisoned *herself*?

RUTH. Accidentally. *Well*, Inspector?

INSPECTOR. Um. I think you may be right.

MARY. Then I needn't come to the police station tonight after all?

INSPECTOR. No, Miss Trellington. There seems no need for it now.

MARTIN. What about the inquest, Inspector?

INSPECTOR (*crossing to the door up* L) I should think it would be quite straightforward.

(MARTIN *moves to* R *of the Inspector*)

Just a confirmation of what we already know. Mrs Prendergast, my congratulations. You've proved yourself a most valuable assistant.

RUTH (*moving up* C) Not at all, Inspector. It was a pleasure. More than that—almost a necessity.

INSPECTOR. Good night.

(*The* INSPECTOR *hiccups loudly and exits up* L)

FAWCETT. And I must be going too. Dear me! Mrs Trellington! What a narrow escape! Good night.

(MR FAWCETT *exits up* L. *The sound of a Christmas carillon is is heard off*)

RUTH. A happy Christmas, everybody.
ALL (*ad lib.*) A happy Christmas.
MARTIN. You know, I think we should all have a drink.

(*After what they have been through, this is too much, and a look of horror comes across their faces, as they sink on to chairs*)

ALL (*ad lib.*) Oh, *no*.

CURTAIN

FURNITURE AND PROPERTY PLOT

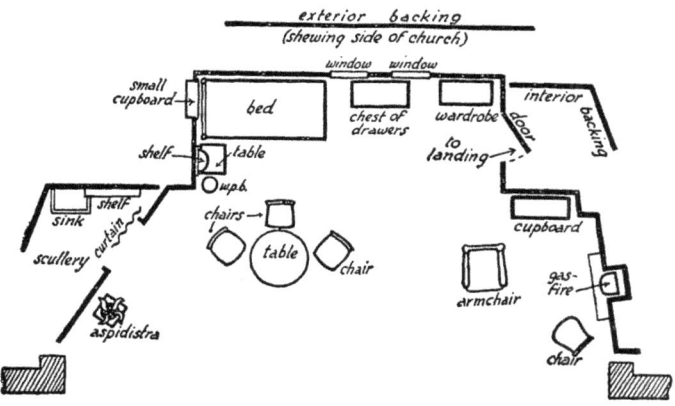

ACT I

On stage: Armchair. *On it:* cushion
Kitchen chair. *On it:* Janet's nightdress
Wardrobe. *On it:* suitcases
Chest of drawers. *On them:* work-basket, handbag with purse containing 1s.
           In drawer: writing case with pad and pen
Cupboard (*above bed*) key in lock
Bedstead. *On it:* bedding, faded rug, cushions, Martin's coat
        On bedpost: hot-water bottle
Bedside table. *On it:* table-lamp, jug of water, tumbler
Circular table. *On it:* cloth, doctor's bag, prescription pad, stethoscope
Waste-paper box
3 dining chairs
China cabinet (*down* R) *In it:* china
Cupboard (*up* L) *In it:* Janet's coat with scarf and gloves in pocket. 3 tumblers on shelf
        On it: hat-box, basket
On mantelpiece: box of matches, bottle of pills, photograph of Lady Glassbury, clock, Christmas cards, ornaments, photographs
Over mantelpiece: oil painting of Edwardian lady
On chair above table: Janet's cardigan
In corner by wardrobe: umbrella

Gas fire
Gas meter
Fender
Window curtains
Door curtain (R)
On window ledges: potted ferns
On walls: framed texts, religious water-colours, photograph of officer
Linoleum and rugs on floor
Over pictures: sprigs of holly
Paper chains
2 electric wall-brackets
Light switch below door up L
In scullery: sink with water tap, gas stove with kettle, plate rack with plates and pans

Window curtains open
Lights on
Gas fire on

Off stage: Tray. *On it:* 2 cups, 2 saucers, 2 spoons, pot of tea, bowl of sugar, jug of milk, plate with cake and knife (JANET)
Packet. *In it:* brooch (FAWCETT)
String bag. *In it:* parcel of fish (LAVINIA)
Parcel. *In it:* 2 half-bottles of whisky (LAVINIA)
Wrapped bottle of medicine (MARY)
Bowl of water (RUTH)

Personal: MARTIN: fountain pen, case with cigarettes, box of matches
FAWCETT: 3 Christmas cards in envelopes, coins
ELEANOR: purse. *In it:* 1s.

ACT II

Empty ¼ whisky out of bottle in cupboard above bed
Window curtains open
Lights off
Gas fire off

Off stage: Christmas card in envelope (MARY)
Slip of paper (INSPECTOR)
3 tumblers (JANET)

ACT III

Window curtains open
Lights on
Gas fire on

Off stage: Small white packet (INSPECTOR)
Trinket box with cheap jewellery and powder box with ring and cyanide in screw of paper in trick compartment (INSPECTOR)

Personal: INSPECTOR: box of mints, handkerchief, wallet with envelope

FAWCETT: spectacles

LIGHTING PLOT

Property fittings required: gas fire, pair electric wall-brackets,
table-lamp (all practical)
light switch below door up L

Interior. An attic bed-sitting-room. The same scene throughout
THE APPARENT SOURCES OF LIGHT are a table-lamp R and 2 electric wall-brackets over the fireplace L
THE MAIN ACTING AREAS are RC, C and LC

ACT I A winter evening
To open: Flood behind backcloth for church window effect
Blue outside windows
Strips outside doors L and R
Fittings on
Gas fire on

Cue 1	JANET moves to fire	(Page 4)
	Fade fire to out	
Cue 2	ELEANOR lights fire	(Page 10)
	Bring in fire	

ACT II Night
To open: The room in darkness
Blue outside windows
Strip outside door L on
Strip outside door R off
Fittings off
Gas fire off

Cue 3	JANET switches on lights	(Page 26)
	Snap in wall-brackets, table-lamp and strip outside door R	
	Bring up on-stage lights	
Cue 4	JANET lights fire	(Page 26)
	Bring in fire	

ACT III Night
To open: Lights as at the end of the previous Act

Cue 5	The INSPECTOR switches off the lights	(Page 48)
	Snap out onstage lights	
	Snap out fittings	
Cue 6	The INSPECTOR switches on the lights	(Page 48)
	Snap on onstage lights	
	Snap on fittings	

EFFECTS PLOT

ACT I

Cue 1	Before the rise of CURTAIN "Carols" *Fade when CURTAIN rises*	(Page 1)
Cue 2	JANET: "Of course." *Church clock strikes the half hour*	(Page 13)
Cue 3	RUTH: "That's right." *Church clock strikes the three-quarters*	(Page 23)
Cue 4	LAVINIA: "I'll get my things at once." *Organ voluntary is heard*	(Page 25)

ACT II

Cue 5	INSPECTOR: ". . . Can I have your guarantee . . ." *Organ voluntary is heard*	(Page 52)
Cue 6	INSPECTOR: ". . . . wouldn't it?" He exits up L. *Church clock strikes the half hour*	(Page 52)
Cue 7	INSPECTOR: "Good night." He exits up L. *A Christmas carillon is heard*	(Pages 65–6)

All these effects have been recorded and are available from Stagesound (London) Ltd, 3 Dansey Place, London, W.1.

www.ingramcontent.com/pod-product-compliance
Ingram Content Group UK Ltd.
Pitfield, Milton Keynes, MK11 3LW, UK
UKHW021840210426
5322IPUK00022B/394